Discover Life!
Not just any life, but a meaningful life!

Johnny F. Pinos

DEDICATION

This book is dedicated to my heavenly Father, who
has sustained me with His love, mercy, and grace in
spite of my rebellion and sin.
To my Lord and Savior, Jesus Christ, who gave His
life so I can have life.
To the Holy Spirit, who with tenderness has helped
me find a life that is worth living.
To my children, Paul, David, Grace, and Joy, whom
I love so dearly.

CONTENTS

PREFACE

The discovery of America by Christopher Columbus on October 12, 1492, would change forever the future of our continent. That discovery became the beginning of the colonization and conquest of America with all of its implications.

In 1879, Thomas Edison, after thousands of experiments, figured out that carbonized paper filament produces a lasting light bulb. Thomas Edison's bulb produced light for almost fifteen hours. Thus, he is credited with producing the first effective and useful incandescent bulb.

In the 1870s, Alexander Graham Bell developed the telephone in his attempt to improve the telegraph.

The discovery of our modern computers in 1945 is attributed to Alan Turing, who took advantage of all the previous knowledge of others and had a fantastic vision of the potential these machines could have, envisioning some of the future applications.

Discoveries have a way of affecting life in dramatic ways. They can be positive ones that enhance our present life, or they can be negative ones that can cause pain and suffering, as the discovery of a malignant tumor in a patient.

What can we do when life throws a heavy blow at our face and we feel devastated by it? The cheap counsel to "think positive" won't do it. Many times the hard realities of life present such a struggle that we become confused, desperate, and even hopeless. That is when we would like to receive comfort and words that would bring some kind of hope to our lives.

That is precisely why I wrote this book. It didn't come from those exciting days of pondering how beautiful life is; instead, it came during those days when I questioned everything: *Does God really exist? If He does exist, does He really care for me? Hasn't He abandoned me? Is life really worth it? Because right now, it really stinks! Maybe things would be better if I didn't exist,* I thought. In fact, I came to the point that I regretted that I was born!

How can you reach that low? In my case, it was my harvest of some terrible choices and decisions I had made. When you see all your world crumbling down, and it keeps on going down, when you think you have hit bottom, then you realize that is not the bottom yet. There is more pain waiting for you.

I had so many questions, but in those days, nowhere to find an answer. Silence is the only answer you get. The sense of abandonment is so painfully real! Desperation comes in. Impotence joins there also. Let's add some depression. You start questioning if you are going insane, or if this is just a terrible nightmare. Then you come to your senses again and realize it is real; it is happening to you.

What can you do? Where do you go? If you dare to talk to someone about your struggles and pain, many well-intentioned people will give you cheap advice: "Just think positive!" or, "Things are going to be okay." Then you feel stupid. Why did you open your big mouth in the first place? It would have been better if you didn't say anything. In one of those moments of excruciating pain and grief, you cry out with the most passionate and fervent prayer you ever made: "God, please stop this suffering. Please take my life away." It is interesting, even that prayer is not answered!

If you have been there, then you may be interested in continuing to read this book. If your life hasn't been as complicated as what I have described, but there is such an emptiness inside of you, a deep sense of dissatisfaction or struggling to make sense of your life, or you just want to make the most of your life, then I invite you to join me and reason with me as I analyze the pursuit of happiness and share with you the principles and suggestions that will help you have a better understanding of life and discover that a more positive, productive, and meaningful life is at your reach. So, discover life!

PART I

LAYING A FOUNDATIONAL UNDERSTANDING

"Johnny, I want to tell you something," said Susan. "What is it, Susan?" I said.

"Do you remember the day you came to my house because my mother had asked you to pay me a visit because I had many problems and was desperate?" she replied.

"Yes, I remember that we had a long conversation that day—what about it?" I said.

"Well," she said, "that day I was planning on killing myself and my two girls because I was overwhelmed with my problems and had no hope left. But that day, God used you in a way that brought peace and hope again to my life."

My heart was filled with joy and gratitude seeing a person on the brink of suicide coming back to a life with hope and a future for herself and her two beautiful daughters. (The name is fictitious for privacy reasons.)

According to the National Center for Health Statistics, a division of the U.S. Department of Health and Human Services, in 2004, suicide was the eleventh leading cause of death in the United States, accounting for 32,637 deaths. The overall rate was 10.9 suicide deaths per 100,000 people.

An estimated eight to twenty-five suicide attempts occur per every suicide death.

This information is sobering! And I know that in the year 2008, the numbers were even greater. There is such a level of desperation, confusion, anxiety, and hopelessness invading the lives of so many. The eradication of absolute truth in our post-modernistic society, where human life is deprived of purpose and meaning, is bringing catastrophic consequences, which brings a cloud of hopelessness to many.

Jesus said, "I have come that they may have life, and have it to the full" (John 10:10b). What a contrast with this new philosophy that is invading our society! But let me ask you, Are you living to the fullest?

Someone has said, "You are what you think," and I would like to add, Your behavior is a result of the convictions you have, or your actions reflect what you really believe. Therefore, your personal worldview, or your way of thinking, or your philosophy of life, as you prefer to call it, is going to affect directly the things you do and the attitudes you have. For this reason, it becomes imperative that you have a good, realistic, and truthful worldview if you attempt to have a life that is abundant with purpose and meaning.

Think with me for a moment. If you are going to build a sturdy, solid house, you need to start with a good foundation because if you disregard that, your house may collapse while you are building or may fold down after you have already moved in. This analogy applies to your life.

There has to be a good foundation, one that is solid, that will endure time and the storms of life that will come your way because, as you know, life is not easy, and you are facing or will face tremendous turmoil. Therefore, intentionally, we need to build our lives in such a way that will stand the struggles of life.

Jesus spoke about this in the parable of the wise and foolish builders in Matthew 7:24-27:

Therefore everyone who hears these words of mine and puts them into practice is like a wise man who built his house on the rock. The rain came down, the streams rose, and the winds blew and beat against that house; yet it did not fall, because it had its foundation on the rock. But everyone who hears these words of mine and does not put them into practice is like a foolish man who built his house on sand. The rain came down, the streams rose, and the winds blew and beat against that house, and it fell with a great crash.

You and I know very well that it is not IF some trials come our way, but rather WHEN those trials come our way. Many years ago, a friend of mine said, "People and adverse circumstances will rob the joy of our lives." That has already happened in your life, and most likely, it will happen again. Therefore, we must put a solid foundation in our lives that will stand those strong winds of pain, suffering, injustice, and tragedy, so when the storms of life hit us, we will have the necessary support to stand firm.

My intention in this part of the book is to lay that foundation in the way of basic principles for life. I want to reason and analyze with you these principles, then you'll need to make a choice or confirm what you already believe.

On the following pages, you will find some views that are going to be challenging at times, and in some cases, you are going to struggle to determine which view or views you are going to accept as a conviction in your life.

Let me clarify what I mean by conviction: It is a strong belief that is so important to you that you have chosen it to be a core value in your life. You have embraced it with all your heart and understanding. It is a principle that you want to live by. In other words, these are not just "nice ideas in your head," but the values you live by.

THE PURSUIT OF HAPPINESS VS. THE OBEDIENCE OF REJOICING

> Delight yourself in the Lord and he will give you the desires of your heart.
>
> Psalm 37:4

Most people are happiness seekers. All of us look for things that satisfy us, that give us pleasure and fulfill our desires. It seems like we were created for happiness. So following our natural instincts and desires, we look for happiness. It is normal behavior to look for happiness. The opposite of that would be the pursuit of suffering, which in psychology is known as MASOCHISM, or pleasure in pain, which is a mental pathology, and no one in his right mind would want that. People are willing to spend everything they have on the pursuit of happiness, and it is exactly on this point that we commit the worst mistakes!

Just consider with me, for the sake of happiness, some fall in bad relationships that destroy them instead of building them up. Some fall prey to bad habits, which wreck their lives, their loved ones, and their future. Some work so hard that they neglect those loved ones they are sacrificing for. Some look for power and find themselves so lonely and empty. Some look for pleasure, and this pleasure, which is supposed to give them happiness, ends up destroying them, including their dignity and self-respect. I could keep on going with this issue, but I think I have made my point.

We need to realize that happiness is circumstantial and very elusive. It depends one hundred percent on the good happenings going on in your favor. Anything different than that is going to cause you discomfort, pain, suffering, frustration, anger, and so on.

So if happiness depends only on good happenings or favorable circumstances, then you don't have too much control over that, because life depends also on others and circumstances out of your hands. No wonder many people get so discouraged with life that they decide to end their misery the fast way, suicide.

Have you ever wondered why some beautiful, famous, and wealthy people end their lives this way? Or why they are so miserable in the first place? We can conclude that fortune, fame, pleasure, and power are not necessarily the right ingredients for happiness. The many dysfunctional, confused, and miserable lives of Hollywood are a clear example of what I'm trying to say.

I have concluded, then, that pursuing happiness as the main goal in life is a poor choice. It is not that the pursuit of happiness is bad in itself, but if that becomes the primary objective in life, or that search for happiness is the driving force of everything you do, then I believe you have chosen the wrong path.

The pursuit of happiness as your main goal is going to bring you pain, suffering, misery, and discouragement sooner or later because you don't really have control of other people, of many of your circumstances, and many times even of yourself. So it is better to stop pursuing happiness as your primary goal, but you should take advantage of every moment of happiness that comes your way. It would be foolish not to enjoy and make the most of those blessings of happy moments.

If the pursuit of happiness is not going to be your main goal in life, then what is going to take its place? Let me propose and challenge you to consider the idea of a commandment in the Bible where the apostle Paul writes: "Rejoice in the Lord always. I will say it again: Rejoice!" (Philippians 4:4). The way that verse is written, it is an imperative, an order, a command. I wonder if we have taken that command as serious as "Thou shalt not lie" or "Thou shalt not kill." It is my perception that many of us did not realize that it was a commandment to be obeyed, or that some of us did not even know that that commandment existed in the first place!

Why would God give us such a command? Could it be that the God who created us had wired us to find satisfaction, pleasure, and fulfillment in His good and perfect will for us? Could it be that when God created the universe and everything on this planet, it was not only to display His power and majesty, but also because He wanted to share that rejoicing with those whom He loved and created in His likeness? I believe God is so interested in us that He provides all we need to have an abundant life here on earth, and that is why there is a command to rejoice.

So what is rejoicing? Webster's dictionary defines it as: "to be glad, to delight, to be happy." My personal definition is that rejoicing is having pleasure and satisfaction in obeying God and bringing Him glory, or, simply, joy is the pleasure and satisfaction of doing something that is pleasing to God, and God, in turn, through His Holy Spirit, puts joy in our hearts that invades our being independent of whatever the circumstances may be. So joy comes from God as a fruit of His Spirit, and it does not depend on the favorable happenings in our lives, but on the generosity of His grace.

At this moment, I would like to dissect a little bit the two verses I have included in this section:

> Delight yourself in the Lord and he will give you the desires of your heart.
>
> Psalm 37:4

> Rejoice in the Lord always. I will say it again: Rejoice!
>
> Philippians 4:4

Since "delight" is a synonym of "rejoice," this verse is quite similar to the expression Paul is using in his letter to the Philippians. So we may ask ourselves: What does it mean to rejoice or delight in the Lord? What comes to mind?

These are some thoughts that come to my mind as I'm pondering this expression:

- It is God, and not my good circumstances, that is the reason for my rejoicing.
- It seems like if I choose God to be my reason for rejoicing, then God is going to do His part, provide the joy that I need. This would make perfect sense when the Scripture says that joy is the fruit of the Holy Spirit (Galatians 5:22).
- Emotions come and go, and many times are not under our control, but obedience is an act of the will independent of emotions.
- Obedience then produces a fruit, or a harvest, in direct relation to the command I'm obeying.
- God is the One who is promising to give us the desires of our hearts. Since His promises are secure, then I can count on the fact that He will accomplish what He has said He will do.

Could this command be obeyed without our complete trust in Him? Do you see the connection here between faith in God and rejoicing in Him? I'm just thinking at this point about the connection between rejoicing in the Lord and the verse Hebrews 11:6: "And without faith it is impossible to please God."

This command to rejoice in the Lord always, how can we obey it?

First we would need to make a decision that from now on and with God's help, we are going to train and discipline our minds to delight in God for who He is, for what He has done, for what He will do, and for what He is to me.

This exercise will teach each of us to be a better worshiper, a more grateful person, and a more positive Christian. This will transform our lives.

Second, we need to delight in obeying all His commands, instead of having a negative attitude that we don't agree with some of His commands or we consider some of them to be a little foolish, like loving our enemies or blessing those who hurt us. We need to keep a submissive attitude and obey in spite of the fact that our desire is not one hundred percent there.

Let me share one experience I had many years ago about this kind of obedience. There was a certain person who was discrediting me and damaging my reputation before many people. When I found out, I was outraged! I was thinking at that moment that if he showed up there, I would make justice with my own fists.

At that moment, I felt a conviction from God that He was telling me, "Johnny, just pray for him." I said to the Lord, "Yea! You punish him right now!" God again talked to my conscience and said, "No, I'm asking you to pray for blessings on his life." I said, "I would be a hypocrite to do that because You know how I feel." Then God said again, "Just do it, please; just obey Me." Then I said, "Okay, Lord, I'll do it; I will obey." Then I prayed for this person.

Nothing magical happened at that moment or the next day, but later on, about two weeks after that prayer, we met face to face on a corner in my hometown. I greeted him, and he greeted me back. Then I saw God's work in my heart. I had such a peace, and instead of anger and hatred, I felt so much love and compassion for this person, which I still feel to this day.

Understanding that His commands are beautiful and perfect because each command describes the nature and attributes of God has helped me to be more submissive to God and to enjoy His fellowship with me. Letting God be

God and being His child have made my relationship with Him stronger and more fruitful.

Also, I'm going to take the time to enjoy His revelation of His existence, His power and wisdom, through everything He has created in this world.

And lastly, I have chosen to enjoy His Word as the love letter He has written to us. I've found that reading and studying His Word not only provides me with truth and guidance, but fills my life with strength and joy, so much so that it is hard to describe it with words.

Let me conclude this part by saying that the obedience of rejoicing in God is far greater than the happiness I can find in temporary happy things. And that is besides the eternal glory that is to come to all of us who know Jesus Christ as our Lord and Savior.

PERSONAL PLEASURE VS. THE GLORY OF GOD

> So whether you eat or drink or whatever you do, do it all for the glory of God.
>
> 1 Corinthians 10:31

A drive for pleasure is an innate part of us. We are wired this way. The senses we possess have a tendency to look for pleasure everywhere we go. For instance, we want to feast our eyes on a beautiful sunset, on the colors of a rainbow, on the exotic beauty of an orchid, or we want to delight our appetite in a good meal or our favorite dessert.

We love listening to our favorite music; in fact, we could be listening for hours and hours if it were not for other things we have to do. Or we may just want to relax by a spring of water, just to hear the water play and to enjoy its relaxing sound. What about the smell that we like to perceive—that special cologne or perfume that intoxicates us, or the aroma of coffee as we enter our home?

It seems like we were created for pleasure through and through. I think no one can argue with that. Even God, after He created everything, said, "IT IS GOOD"! There was this great sense of pleasure and accomplishment. So where is pleasure going wrong? If God made so many things for us to enjoy, where is it that pleasure becomes something negative and even destructive?

There are some principles that we need to consider.

1. **God should be the One in whom we find more pleasure than in anyone or anything else.** He should be the first and foremost Source of pleasure we have. If that is not happening, then something or someone is taking His place. I don't think a wife would be so thrilled knowing that her husband finds more pleasure in some other woman at his workplace. Likewise, God is not going to be pleased if we put someone or something in His place. God said, "Love the Lord your God with all your heart and with all your soul and with all your strength" (Deuteronomy 6:5), and, in Psalm 37:4, said, "Delight yourself in the Lord and he will give you the desires of your heart."

The understanding that God is exclusive on this should be something we need to evaluate in our lives. May it not be said of us, "These people praise Me with their lips, but their hearts are far away from Me."

Isaiah 43:7 says: ". . . everyone who is called by my name, whom I created for my glory, whom I formed and made."

First Corinthians 10:31 says, "So whether you eat or drink or whatever you do, do it all for the glory of God."

The two passages clearly state the main reason for our existence. A lack of understanding in this area will make us selfish or idolaters, or even both.

2. **God created all things for our pleasure and use, but we need to use them and delight in them according to the standards He has established for our good.**

   Here are some examples:

   - Enjoy your food, but don't stuff yourself (gluttony) to the point that you feel sick and risk your own health.
   - Enjoy sex within the boundaries of marriage so you don't have to suffer the consequences of guilt, shame, venereal disease, unwanted pregnancy, abortion, loss of respect, broken homes, broken relationships, and so on.
   - Enjoy dessert *after* you have eaten a *good* meal (especially for kids).
   - Enjoy your clothes; just don't dress in a way that you provoke others to sin, or you make a fool of yourself.

Any pleasure used outside of God's standards will damage our relationship with Him, with others, and even with ourselves. I know enough people, including myself, who hate themselves because they did stupid things in their pursuit of pleasure. In many cases, we will destroy ourselves. Just read the newspaper or turn on the TV, and you will find the reality of what I'm saying.

Pleasure should not become the purpose of our lives because it will make us his slaves, and we will get what we didn't bargain for.

Pleasure should be something we enjoy as life unfolds, and we need to make sure the pleasure we are experiencing honors and glorifies God; if not, most likely, it will damage or destroy us, and it will damage our fellowship with God.

We need to consider at this time that we have three powerful enemies that will do whatever it takes to give you pleasure outside of God's parameters and will. These enemies rage within and outside of ourselves. They are the world, the flesh, and the devil.

We need to understand the world as a system that opposes the will of God and the truth of His Word. For instance, the world tries to dictate your value by the things you possess. Another example would be: "It is okay to believe in God, but don't become so fanatical, putting God in everything you do."

The flesh is the natural tendency that all of us have to do things out of our instincts, but opposed to the will of God. For instance, I think I'm going to tell this lie to get out of this problem I am facing right now. Another example: "I know I am stuffed, but it tastes so good, I'm going to have just a little more."

The mission of the devil, God's archenemy, is to destroy everything God wants to build and go against everything God says. For example, he'll tell us, "Just do it this time; no one will find out, and you will be okay," or, "There is nothing wrong with what you want to do. There are only those religious freaks that want to brainwash you. In fact, the majority of people are doing it; therefore, it cannot be too bad."

These enemies we will have to face day in and day out. Of course, God has given us victory over them if we depend on Him and apply simple obedience to His truth.

I have discovered that I can enjoy the pleasures of life better if I don't pursue pleasure, but instead seek to glorify God with everything I do or think. Finding my pleasure in Him, He turns and blesses me more than what I can think or imagine.

One last thought on this matter. I have found that people who pursue pleasure not only make more mistakes, but become selfish, egocentric, and sometimes even foolish.

LIVING FOR YOURSELF VS. DYING DAILY

Whoever finds his life will lose it, and whoever loses his life for my sake will find it.

Matthew 10:39

Here again, we are going to face another characteristic of human nature, and that is that our tendency is to put ourselves first in everything. Let me illustrate this point with some examples:

- You think, *Wouldn't it be nice if the rest of the people at home prepare the food I really like all the time, instead of my having to 'sacrifice' myself with food I don't care for? Or if everybody would leave me alone with my favorite show instead of others trying to change the channel or stop the movie I'm watching?*
- Have you noticed that babies, and kids in general, don't care if you are tired, exhausted, or depressed? What they want is right now! What about those kids who don't let you spend some peaceful time in your visits, and instead keep annoying you with their demands?
- *If they could only change that annoying music at work or in the restaurant or in the supermarket!* you think.
- *Wouldn't it be paradise if everything worked just the way I want?*
- A lovely lady was telling this to her best friend: "Charles is amazing! He listens to me, he understands me, he tells me that I am so special, he gives me nice gifts, he takes me to different places, and he spends most of his time with me. He even tells me that he thinks of me all the time. Isn't he so wonderful?" Please note the ME pronoun in this paragraph.

25

So, from birth to death, we cannot deny that we would like things our way. What is wrong with this? God's perspective! He wants us to deny ourselves and to put God and then others ahead of us. God has so much wisdom in this small concept because if we have all things our way, we would become extremely egotistical, selfish, arrogant, proud, insensitive, egocentric, and even foolish.

This act of denying ourselves brings out the best in us. Besides, by pleasing and honoring God, we will develop a character that is influential, humble, wise, generous, respectful, delightful, and so on. Just think for a moment: What do you think of someone who has a servant's attitude, and is unselfish, generous, gentle, and humble? If you were like me, you would think very highly of such a person. I would have tremendous respect and admiration for a person like that. Why not, then, become that kind of person and leave a legacy for those around us?

I want to challenge you to be a person who on a daily basis denies himself and searches for all the ways he can bring glory to God. Then you will discover a secret for an abundant and fulfilling life.

Bear in mind that this needs to become a daily discipline. It does not come automatically, but once you train yourself in this area, you will notice that there is more to life than what you thought. Don't expect that with one prayer, God is going to touch you, and you will be selfless for the rest of your life. No! You will need to make a personal choice and decision every single day.

Jesus gave us His example. By literally giving His life for our sake and living a life to honor His Father in heaven, now He is glorified above any name or power in heaven and on earth.

When He was here on earth, He said: "If anyone would come after me, he must deny himself and take up his cross [a symbol of death] and follow me. For whoever wants to save his life will lose it, but whoever loses his life for me will find it" (Matthew 16:24-25).

He knows your needs because He created you. You will discover that what you are REALLY looking for is the same as God's perfect and pleasant will for your life. In perfect fellowship, God wants to give you the real things that make your life meaningful and abundant.

But you need to trust Him one hundred percent because He has your best interest in His heart and His mind. Without faith it is IMPOSSIBLE TO PLEASE GOD.

THE PURSUIT OF POWER VS. THE JOY OF SERVICE

> And whoever wants to be first must be your slave.
>
> Matthew 20:27

Megalomania is a sick or obsessive drive for power. We have seen or heard in our times or in history of people like Adolph Hitler, Idi Amin, Saddam Hussein, Mao Tze Dong, Nero, plus an endless list of tyrants who controlled people with such disrespect, cruelty, and contempt.

Abuse of authority we find everywhere, in government, businesses, church organizations, the military, police departments, judges, workplaces, homes, and more.

How devastating and painful it is to hear of the cry of so many victims as they share the madness of our society in the area of abuse and tyranny. Why is that?

As we saw in the previous point, humankind has an innate desire to have everything under his control. Unfortunately, there is also in human nature this desire for power and recognition. Of course, not all of this is evil. For example:

- A teacher needs a level of authority in order to maintain order in the classroom to be able to share his/her knowledge or accomplish the program that has been preestablished.

- A policeman needs authority to restore peace in the midst of a conflict among two parties.
- A parent needs authority to train his/her child in the right way.

Therefore, there is a need for power and authority in many instances for the well-being of all of us. The lack of power and authority would lead us to chaos and anarchy, where everybody does whatever he wants with complete impunity.

Since we humans have a problem with this issue of power and authority, God has established some principles that will help us relate with one another. The major problem with this area has to do with our attitude and understanding of power.

Authority is the right to rule; power is the ability to rule. God has given us both, but to be used in accordance with His will and for His purposes, which are for the benefit of those around us, not to put us on a pedestal of superiority, but instead to serve others. Any other use of power or authority for our own selfish reasons becomes tyranny toward others.

The misuse of power and authority has to do to a great extent with our significance. The more uncomfortable we feel about ourselves, the more we want to compensate it with power, so we are *over* others and not *under*. Feeling superior is better than feeling inferior, of course! But once again, God teaches us His paradoxes: If you want to be first, then you must become a slave. You may think, *That is not a nice thing to say. Don't you know how important I am?*

God has called us to be His servants, or "slaves," and also to serve one another. This concept of slavery is not easy to understand because in our modern society, there isn't slavery as an accepted and legal status. In the time of Jesus, however, slavery was common, to the point that there were levels of slavery. The lowest slaves were called, in Greek, *doulos*, which means a person with no rights, because his/her owner had ALL the rights over that person. What does that have to do with this point I'm trying to make? It is simply that when Jesus said we need to become slaves, He used the term *doulos*, or the lowest kind of servant, with no rights.

God is asking us to consider ourselves as servants of God and servants of others. If we do this and take this position and attitude, then we will see our lives in a different light. Our lives then become an instrument to serve God and others in every way we can. The first thing that will happen is that pride will be thrown out the window, to open up some room for humility. Our attitude of "me first" and "I'm superior" also will experience a great transformation. God then will use our attitude to lift us up, and He will exalt us; otherwise, we are just making it more difficult for ourselves as we maintain our pride and arrogance.

I submit to you that having the attitude of a servant is not something that diminishes the dignity of a person. On the contrary it enhances the value of a person. Let's say you are talking to a senator in his office, and he treats you in a way that makes you feel that you are more important than he is. Let's say he even invites you for lunch, and he pays the bill at the restaurant. What would you think of that senator? Would he have your vote next time? Would you tell others about your experience with him? What would others think of this senator because of you? You see, being a servant is a good investment!

How much more is it if we think of our Lord Jesus! He, being God Himself, the King of kings and Lord of lords, chose as His close friends a bunch of people who had no reputation, worked as a carpenter, slept wherever He could, washed the feet of his friends, and, ultimately, gave his life as if he were a bad criminal. No wonder so many loved him so that they were willing to give their lives for Him.

Could you imagine how your home would be if everyone wanted to be a servant of the other. Wives would be in shock! Parents, seeing their kids in humble submission and obedience, would think that they are dreaming or that somehow they are already in heaven! Just to make a point, if you are a parent, what would you do for your child who acts as a servant toward you? If you are a spouse, how would you take this attitude of your spouse? Now, apply this concept wherever you go. What do you think is going to happen?

My personal challenge to you: Come down from your pedestal. Risk everything, consider yourself a servant to those around you (by personal experience, I know that many won't understand what you are doing. Some may think you are nuts, or you are too weak), then let God do His part. I'll guarantee, you will be pleasantly surprised, even though it may take a little while.

Bear this in mind: This world is not fair, but let God be the One who smiles at you. The applause of heaven is far greater and more lasting than the recognition of men. MAKE A CHOICE!

> But he gives us more grace. That is why Scripture says: "God opposes the proud but gives grace to the humble.
>
> James 4:6

DEALING WITH ADVERSITY AND SUFFERING

> Consider it pure joy, my brothers, whenever you face trials of many kinds, because you know that the testing of your faith develops perseverance. Perseverance must finish its work so that you may be mature and complete, not lacking anything.
>
> James 1:2-4

It is so easy to talk about rejoicing when things are going fairly well and when we are not facing big problems. We know life is not perfect. Some problems here and there is okay; we kind of expect that. But when you face big problems, not only big, but huge problems and difficulties, then please don't come with these simple spiritual recipes for success and abundant life! Because it is not going to work!

When you feel overwhelmed and impotent under the magnitude of these bad circumstances, the pain is so deep and excruciating that it seems like even God has abandoned us.

That is the way I felt at times, and it is precisely those kinds of days that God used to shape and transform me by His grace. It is after going through that kind of tunnel that I got the idea of writing this book. During those days, I didn't think I would be coming through. The worst thing about those days is that you become very lonely and hopeless. In fact, some haven't been able to make it and have given in to despair. Some have checked out through suicide, others through addictions, and others have rebelled completely against God and have become atheists or have become involved in the occult.

So where are you now?

Let me share with you some thoughts on this matter of adversity and suffering. After that, I would like to reason with you using the text at the beginning of this subject.

- After men sinned against God, this world became filled with injustice, pain, suffering, sickness, death, and so on.
- Men, instead of accepting their responsibility and repenting from their rebellion, raised their hands in rebellion and started putting the blame on God.
- Besides men's wickedness, there is a real enemy of God and ours who hates us passionately, who loves

to cause wars and turmoil among the sons of men, then he hides and with a cynical smile contemplates how we humans point our accusatory fingers to our Creator, who loves us so much that He gave His only Son for us ungrateful people.

- This world is so hostile to God and His people and will do anything to discredit God and despise those who belong to Him.
- Many times we are expecting this world to be the place of love, peace, justice, and understanding, then we face the reality of a world corrupted through and through.
- In difficult situations, we don't realize that many times it is just the harvest of our wrong decisions or the consequences of our wrong behavior.
- That suffering is part of the life this side of life. We are only passing by here. Eternity and glory are waiting for us on the other side.
- Jesus Himself went through such agony when He knew the injustice and all the sin He was going to carry upon Himself. He was wondering if there was another way. For our sake, there wasn't, and that is why He decided to go through anyway up to His death.
- When He was on the cross, He became our sin, and at that moment, His own Father could not look at Him. Then He cried, "My God, My God, why have You forsaken Me?" When I ponder this, my worst suffering pales in comparison to His suffering.
- He knows what it is to go through indescribable suffering.

Now let's look at these verses in James 1.

Consider it pure joy, my brothers, whenever you face trials of many kinds, because you know that the testing of your faith develops perseverance. Perseverance must finish its work so that you may be mature and complete, not lacking anything.

Suffering is part of our lives. It is not a matter of IF we have trials, but WHEN we have trials. That means we have to be prepared for those days. Most of us would agree and say, "I was not prepared for this." In a way, you cannot prepare for these situations, but in another way, yes, we can be prepared for trials and tribulations. Actually, when those situations come, you will discover the "real you." In other words, how you react to the adversities of life shows you who you are and what your convictions are.

I was told a story that in a country where Christians were forbidden to have religious services, one day unexpectedly, two guards came into a meeting with automatic weapons in their hands. As they interrupted their meeting, they said, "We know you are Christians that are meeting here illegally in spite of the order that you cannot do that, but we are going to give you an opportunity to save your lives."

"Whoever denies his faith in this Jesus can go home freely, and we will spare your life," they said, and they gave some time for them to take advantage of the offer. Some of them left, denying their faith, but some of them stayed there anyway. The guards closed the door behind them, and once they were alone, they told the Christians there, "We love the Lord, too, but wanted to be together with those who were real Christians," and then they hugged each other and wept together.

When trials come our way, God has a plan and a desire for us: He wants to shape our character and make us stronger than before. Remember that God wants to conform us to the image of His Son, Jesus Christ (Romans 8:29). Also, He wants to teach us some lessons that we would not get otherwise. In my personal experience, I have been able to pay more attention to God in the midst of pain than in the comfort of life. Suffering makes us more sensitive. Somebody has said, "When you hit bottom, you can only look up."

There is an advantage when you are broken; you are in a position of humility and really want help. Looking at my life, I wouldn't trade my days of pain and sorrow for anything else in this world. Those were the days when in desperation and confusion, I cried for God from the depths of my soul, and in due time, God answered me. The answers do not come automatically, right at the moment you want, but when the storm is over, you will see God's wisdom and how carefully He was working with you. When there are questions that haven't been answered yet, you may feel very uncomfortable and disappointed. That is when you need to trust God more than ever, and He will give you His peace.

The main lesson I get from this passage in James is that trials will produce perseverance and endurance, and then having obtained them, they produce maturity and completeness. We as parents want our kids to grow up and become mature so we can rest, knowing that they can handle life well. In the same way, God wants to see that we reach a level of maturity so that we can handle life well for ourselves and also so we can assist others. This way we glorify God and are useful to those around us, starting in our own homes.

If you are facing trials right now, please ask yourself these questions:

- Is the trial I'm going through the result of my own sin?
- Is it a test of my faith, and is God trying to teach me something?

- Am I a victim of the evil and injustice of this world?
- What is the attitude God wants me to display?
- How am I going to glorify God in all of this?
- What is my testimony or example to those who are watching me?

Compare your life to a diamond. God wants to make it of greater value. What is the impurity that is holding you back? Or what is the virtue God wants to develop in you?

I would like to recommend some books that I believe will be a blessing to you as you struggle with suffering:

- *When God Doesn't Make Sense,* by Dr. James Dobson
- *Where Is God When It Hurts,* by Philip Yancey
- *A Grief Observed,* by C.S. Lewis

LIVING TODAY IN PERSPECTIVE OF ETERNITY

Do not store up for yourselves treasures on earth, where moth and rust destroy, and where thieves break in and steal. But store up for yourselves treasures in heaven, where moth and rust do not destroy, and where thieves do not break in and steal. For where your treasure is, there your heart will be also.

Matthew 6:19-21

Today's philosophy, "Eat, drink, and be happy, for tomorrow we will die," has been growing in our modern society at a very fast pace, especially among youth. This has affected the Christian church in general. We have lost the perspective that we were created with eternity in our hearts. I believe we need more than ever to come back to the words of Jesus in Matthew chapter 6.

I wonder if some of us are just satisfied with the knowledge that because of the sacrifice of Christ on our behalf, we will make it to heaven, and forget that there is more to it than just "going to heaven."

We know that salvation is a free gift from God to all who put their trust in Him, but why is it that the Bible mentions rewards, retribution, crowns, and treasures in heaven?

Salvation is a gift for all who have accepted Christ as Lord and Savior, and we know that no one deserves it, so why does the Bible speak of prizes or rewards?

It is because everything we do here on earth has a consequence or retribution in heaven. You and I know that we cannot do one deed to deserve heaven, but God wants for us to "store up . . . treasures in heaven." Eternal life in heaven is what God wants to give us to share in His presence, but also He wants to recognize our labor for His glory.

He is an extremely generous Lord, who is not satisfied with just giving us eternal life in heaven and personal fellowship with Him. On top of that, He wants to give us opportunities for "extra prizes," and that is where we can be wise investors of our lives and good stewards of everything God has given us: time, talents, capacities, gifts, finances, opportunities.

How do we store up treasures in heaven?

Everything you do in His name and for His glory counts toward those treasures. All the effort, dedication, love, generosity, responsibility, and creativity you use will be deposits you are making in "your savings account" in heaven and for eternity.

Please bring to mind those different passages where Jesus explained on different occasions what He pays special attention to:

- If you are persecuted for His name, you will be rewarded in heaven (Matthew 5:11-12).

- If you give to the needy, He will reward you (Matthew 6:1-4).
- If you pray, He will reward you (Matthew 6:5-6).
- If you fast, He will reward you (Matthew 6:16-18).
- If you help widows and orphans in their distress, He will reward you (James 1:27).
- If you give a cup of water to someone, He will reward you (Mark 9:41).
- If you persevere under trial, He will reward you (James 1:12).

As you can see, these are only some examples that demonstrate that God wants to reward you for what you do for Him. Of course, you know if you do such things for your own glory or for the recognition from men, then that recognition is all that you will get, but not from God.

Any investment you make for God's kingdom will be rewarded. When your works are judged in heaven, wouldn't it be nice and overwhelming to hear Jesus say, "Well done, good and faithful servant"? Please live a life that counts for Him. I have told the Lord, "I don't want to waste the days I have left here anymore. Please make them count for Your glory."

There is nothing wrong with working to provide for your needs and for your loved ones, but if that is all you are doing, when are you going to start making investments in heaven? Remember, after you die, it is too late. The window of opportunity will be closed.

There is a nice little book on this subject by Dr. Bruce Wilkinson called *A Life God Rewards*. I strongly recommend reading it.

LOVE: THE TEST YOU NEED TO PASS

> Dear friends, let us love one another, for love comes
> from God. Everyone who loves has been born of
> God and knows God. Whoever does not love does
> not know God, because God is love.
>
> 1 John 4:7-8

In Matthew 22:37-40, Jesus said: "'Love the Lord your God with all your heart and with all your soul and with all your mind.' This is the first and greatest commandment. And the second is like it: 'Love your neighbor as yourself.' All the Law and the Prophets hand on these two commandments."

From these two passages listed here, we can conclude that loving God and loving others is extremely important for us if we say we know God. Otherwise, we are just fooling ourselves.

"Love" is a word that is used in so many ways. It can be as profound as loving your child, or it can be so superficial, as my daughter would say, "I love pizza." With the same word, you can communicate a deep affection, or simply that you like something. Some love songs that we hear on the radio communicate love as a desire to have the other person, but with no implication of a relationship or a commitment. For this reason, we need to define first what we mean when we are using the term "LOVE" when it relates to God and when it relates to fellow human beings.

Many of us mistakenly think of love more as an emotion, but actually, it is more of an action. Yes, there will be emotions, undoubtedly, but since it is a command, it has more to do with what you do than what you feel. Let me give you this example: You are finally sleeping after a hectic day, and your infant child starts crying at 2 A.M. Half asleep, you get up and change your child's diaper, feed him, put him in bed, then you go back to bed. Don't you think that that is true love? What kind of emotional feelings did you have?

According to the passage at the beginning of this point, we must love God with all our heart, with all our soul, and with all our mind. One of the key words here is ALL, which implies something total or to the fullest. When you give something that is total, or *all*, that means you are left with nothing else. If you have $10,000 in the bank, and you write a check for $10,000, your bank account is left with a zero-dollar balance. Why is it that God wants for you to love with all your heart, with all your soul, and with all your mind? I submit to you that the reasons why God wants this is because:

- He is the only true God, and He deserves all.
- If we don't give all to Him, then we are keeping something for ourselves.
- He wants all because He has something special for us.
- What He has for us will satisfy our needs and what we need to give others and even beyond that.
- One thing I have discovered is that when we give our all to God without reservations, He will open His arms and bless us in ways we have never imagined.

That is why He is asking us to love Him with all the areas of our lives: heart, soul, and mind, which are the deepest expressions of a human being.

I have seen when a Christian loves God the way God is asking him or her to, that the Christian has more love for each member of his or her family and for all of those around him or her. This is also a paradox. Give it all to God, and you will have even more.

One of the things I have realized is that love, like a song says, hurts. True love is extremely risky. You become vulnerable to those you love, and they can hurt you in so many ways: They can betray you, they can lie to you, and they can abandon you, sometimes with a reason, and many times without one. They can leave you in tremendous loneliness, and they can hurt you really bad.

I bet at this moment, you are agreeing with me with a lot of pain in your heart. Some of them will be ungrateful to you, especially after you have done so much for them. I would dare to say that maybe you have been hurt so much that you decided it is not worth giving so much to receive so much pain and suffering in return.

Some of you may be like me, and may have decided that you were not going to risk anymore. I built up walls around me so no one could touch me anymore, and no one could hurt me. I will be as cold as ice if necessary, but I don't want any more pain. I'll keep a prudent distance, and, of course, I'll be prudent and will mistrust everyone.

Did it work? Not really! Because now I feel more lonely than ever, and I keep being hurt anyway! What a miserable life!

How do I pass this test?

A clear understanding of what love is will help us to get on track and have a vision for our personal life. Let me take you through 1 Corinthians 13:4-7: "Love is patient, love is kind. It does not envy, it does not boast, it is not proud. It is not rude, it is not self-seeking, it is not easily angered, it keeps no record of wrongs. Love does not delight in evil but rejoices with the truth. It always protects, always trusts, always hopes, always perseveres." Let me put these fifteen characteristics in a list format and try to clarify each one of them a little more.

- "Love is patient." You have the ability to accept suffering for the sake of the other person, and have tolerance in the midst of annoying attitudes or behavior.

- "Love is kind." You are gentle and with a predisposition to do all the good that is possible.
- "It does not envy." You rejoice in the accomplishment and victories of the other person, and are not jealous of the good things that come to the other person.
- "It does not boast." You don't want to show off or impress others with your abilities or success so others may think how important you are.
- "It is not proud." You don't have the attitude of being superior to the other person and are willing to recognize your faults and mistakes.
- "It is not rude." Instead, you are polite and well-mannered, treat others with respect and dignity, and do not act offensive and sarcastic, even when you are provoked.
- "It is not self-seeking." Instead, you maintain a servant's attitude because you do not think that people owe you, but you are called to serve others.
- "It is not easily angered." You do not let anger control you, but you pause and meditate on if your answer or action and attitude are going to promote peace or more conflict, and choose peace. If you must confront, you will do it with love, truth, and humility.
- "It keeps no record of wrongs." You remind yourself that you have no right to bring something up if you have already forgiven that person for his or her fault.
- "Love does not delight in evil." You won't put the other person in a position to do something wrong, and if the other person has done something wrong, you won't condone it.

- Love "rejoices with the truth." You find delight in the presence of truth, even if sometimes it becomes uncomfortable.
- "It always protects." You will do whatever is in your power to protect the other person from damage and danger, so the other person can trust in you that you have the best intentions for him or her in mind.
- Love "always trusts." You think the best of the other person, before misjudging, you ask honest questions to find out the truth, always giving an opportunity for the other person to defend himself or herself.
- Love "always hopes." You do not give up, but continue to give opportunities to the other person to improve.
- Love "always perseveres." You have consistency and endurance. You will be there for the long haul.

Looking at this list, you may realize, like I did, that there is no way I can acquire all of those characteristics on my own. If you came to that conclusion, you are right! We humans don't have the ability or capacity to love in such a perfect way. That kind of love is divine, not for fallen creatures like me. That is because that is the kind of love God has for us, and the amazing thing is that God is expecting us to love that way also. How can God ask of us such a task? Because He has poured in us His Holy Spirit, and He will enable us to love that way.

In my personal experience, I had to come out of my cocoon and say to God: "I'm willing to risk everything, and if I have to be hurt over and over again, so be it; and if I have to make a fool of myself, then I will take that also, but please teach me to love the way You want me to. I want to finish my days knowing how to love."

After that prayer, many things didn't turn out the way I would have wanted, but day to day, I'm learning what it is to truly love, and I must confess that life is much more abundant when you put your life at risk for the sake of others.

It does not end there, but God wants us to love in very difficult situations. What about loving our enemies? Just think for a moment of the person who has hurt you the most or has caused you or a loved one the most damage. Here again, you will find out that this command is impossible to obey with our limited human strength. At least three ingredients you will need to have in order to obey God in this area are:

1. Your recognition that you cannot love your enemies on your own.
2. A desire to love in obedience to God and for His glory.
3. Total surrender to God so He can take control of your life and produce in you this fruit of His Spirit.

When you have learned to love your enemies, you also will learn to love those that are not your enemies, but are an annoyance in your life. They can be in your neighborhood, at work, at school, at church, in your family, and so on.

PART II

THE MAJOR KILL-JOYS

Have you ever had problems with termites? I have! I remember some years ago, I had a chair that looked as normal as the other five chairs in the dining room. One day as someone was sitting on that chair, there was a cracking noise, and the seat caved in. I picked up the chair to see what had happen, and as I turned the chair upside down, I realized the wood frame was porous, and lots of dust came out of that chair. That chair became useless because of the termites. Immediately, I started checking the other "normal" chairs, and with disappointment, I found out that two other chairs were in the same bad situation, so I had to burn those chairs in order not to spread termites in other areas.

Many lives have been attacked by "termites." In some instances, those "termites" are easy to detect; other times, they go undetected. Something to ponder is the fact that these termites do "an inside job" in the deepest parts of the soul.

We need to do something about it! With real termites, there are professionals in the extermination of these insects; we call them exterminators, and they are very familiar with how to detect these insects and how to destroy them. But what about these "termites" in our lives?

In this part of the book, we will look at some of these "termites," which are negative influences in life that tend to disharmonize and disrupt us by taking away the joy, hope, and peace that all of us would like to experience in our daily lives. These are roadblocks that stop us from enjoying life to its full potential.

I am describing these "termites" as **kill-joys**, and as I analyze these negative influences, also, I want to propose some solutions in hopes that they would become tools that you can use to overcome the kill-joys of your life. I will attempt not to give you simplistic recipes to confront big and complicated issues, but hopefully some principles to apply and some biblical truth in the confidence that God's truth sets people free.

I pray that God through His Holy Spirit will use some of these tools and bring freedom and victory in some areas of your life. In fact, I have prayed that this book will be an instrument to bring glory to God, and be useful by His grace to touch an important part of your life.

THE LACK OF ASSURANCE OF SALVATION

> I write these things to you who believe in the name of the Son of God so that you may know that you have eternal life.
>
> 1 John 5:13

In my years of counseling, I have found a good percentage of Christians struggling with this issue of assurance of salvation. Some of them feel so defeated and discouraged in their walk with God that they are very close to giving it up.

This theme is very exciting to me, first, because I remember how much I struggled with this issue of assurance of salvation from my teen years to my mid-twenties, and also because I have seen over and over again how a Christian with a lack of assurance of salvation gets overwhelmed and transformed with the discovery that there is certainty and that you can know for sure that you have eternal life and that your eternity is secured.

If you are not certain that you have eternal life, and if you were to die today, you are not sure you will go to heaven, then let me ask you first if you have come to a place in your life where you have recognized that you have sinned against God and that you are lost, then you have repented of your sins and have asked Jesus to come into your life to forgive your sins based on the fact that He died on the cross for you, paying for your sins so you may have peace with God. If so, God not only has forgiven you, but He has given you the gift of eternal life to enjoy with Him forever.

If you realize that you have never done that, then right now, you can do this:

- Confess to God that you have sinned against Him.
- Repent of all the sins you have committed in your life—those that you remember, and those that you don't remember.
- Believe that Jesus paid for all your sins on the cross and that He rose again from the grave to give you eternal life.
- Invite Jesus to come into your life, and ask Him to take control of your life.
- Then give thanks to God for doing what you have just asked.

Now you need to know that there are many benefits God has for you because you have repented of your sins and have trusted God with your life:

- God has become your Father, and you are now His beloved and special child.

- You have been reconciled with God, and now you can enjoy a close relationship and start discovering how amazing and great God is.
- God now lives in you to protect you, to guide you, to comfort you, to correct you, to show you His perfect will for your life, to fill you with His presence, and so on.
- You now have eternal life and the right to go to heaven. The most important part of eternal life is not that you are going to heaven, but that you can have a fantastic fellowship (close friendship and intimacy) with God Himself!
- Your name is written now in heaven in God's book of life.
- All your sins have been forgiven.
- You are a new creation of God. He is transforming you and will continue to do so until you go to His presence.
- You belong to God's family and will be able to relate with all of those who had your same experience.

Now you can start enjoying this new beginning with God. You will have the rest of your life to experience God's goodness and faithfulness, and the opportunity to get to know Him more and more.

If you are a Christian who has already accepted Christ as your Lord and Savior, but are struggling with this issue of assurance of salvation, let me share with you some questions I have had myself and some that I have heard from other Christians:

If I die suddenly with a sin or sins I haven't confessed and repented of yet, would I be saved or condemned?

I don't think there is a Christian who can remember all the sins he or she has committed, and also, I don't think it is possible for us to notice and realize all the sins we commit. There are some sins that have taken me years to realize, and I'm wondering how many of them I still don't realize. That is why I believe that none of us can face death confessing and repenting of all the sins that we have committed. How good it is to know that Jesus paid for all my sins, those committed in the past, those committed in the present, and those that will be committed in the future.

Jesus said when He was dying on the cross, "It is finished!" That expression means complete or paid off to the last cent. With His death, He purchased our complete salvation.

Let's look at some other verses, Hebrews 10:10, 14: "And by that will, we have been made holy through the sacrifice of the body of Jesus Christ once for all. . . . Because by one sacrifice he has made perfect forever those who are being made holy." Jesus cannot die again for you or for anyone else. If His sacrifice covers only your past sins, those committed only until now, then you and I wouldn't have any hope. That is why Jesus' sacrifice is complete and sufficient. That is why I'm so thankful that He paid for all my sins!

Does that mean that I can live my life however I want from now on, since all my sins are already covered?

No! Because if you want a license to sin so freely, then you haven't repented at all of your sins. That also means you don't mind at all being a slave to sin. Part of the evidence of a true believer is that he doesn't want to sin anymore because a Christian wants to live a life that pleases God. If that desire is not in you, then you don't belong to God. You don't know Him yet.

Let me tell you, all Christians sin because all of us have weaknesses until we reach heaven. But it is not because we don't care about sinning, but because we are not perfect, as God is, so we still fail Him.

When I sin, I feel so ashamed, and it seems like God is no longer with me. Could it be that God abandons me when I sin?

Not at all! When we sin, our fellowship is damaged, but God keeps being your Father, and you His beloved child. Your parents didn't say you are not their child when you disobeyed them. They would confront you or correct you, but they didn't disown you every time you failed. Of course, there was tension, and there were some bad feelings and sometimes some uncomfortable consequences, but you remained their child, still eating at their table and living at their home (of course, I'm referring to a normal home, because nowadays, there are homes where a child is not safe).

If one of my kids has disobeyed me, he or she may not feel confident enough to ask me for a special privilege if he or she hasn't resolved his or her fault with me. Or in some cases, this child may have lost some privileges, but my responsibility for his or her needs continues in spite of his or her behavior. If I, being a human, do those things, how much more does our heavenly Father? As soon as my child has apologized, then the fellowship is reestablished, and I'm ready again to bless and serve my kids to the best of my ability.

When a child of God sins, it does not affect his or her salvation because that has already been paid for, but the communion or fellowship with the Father is damaged, and we may lose blessings in the meantime. So repent of your sins and confess them to God so fellowship will be restored and you won't be missing all the blessings God wants to give you. He longs to have perfect harmony with you.

Remember, salvation does not depend on your good works. Ephesians 2:8-9 says, "For it is by grace you have been saved, through faith—and this not from yourselves, it is the gift of God—not by works, so that no one can boast." Good works, instead, is a demonstration that you have salvation.

If I am honest with you, sometimes I don't feel I'm saved at all!

We humans are very emotional, and what we feel at times seems so real that it becomes very hard to differentiate between what is real and what is not. Yes, I have been there many times! Let me ask you, How much is 2+2? You say, "4, of course!" Right! But what if you are very angry and frustrated? You still will say, "It's 4," but what if you are very depressed? How will you answer, How much is 2+2? You will say again, "It is 4." Why is this answer the same in spite of your emotions? Because the FACTS don't change because of emotions. They remain the same. When you KNOW A FACT, that is the way it is, period!

Salvation is a fact from God that you need to know, and not something you need to feel. It is true that sometimes I *feel* that I'm saved, but more than that, I KNOW that I am saved and that I have eternal life! You may be asking, "How do you know that for sure?" I am glad you asked! Look what it says in 1 John 5:13: "I write these things to you who believe in the name of the Son of God so that you may know that you have eternal life."

I don't pretend that I have answered all your questions in regards to assurance of salvation, but I pray that some of the biblical evidence I have presented here may have helped you in some way. May God give you the certainty you need.

LOW SELF-IMAGE

For by the grace given me I say to every one of you: Do not think of yourself more highly than you ought, but rather think of yourself with sober judgment, in accordance with the measure of faith God has given you.

Romans 12:3

To see yourself more highly than what you really are is self-deception, pride, and arrogance. To look at yourself lower than what you really are is called the inferiority complex and hinders you from the potential you have to offer. Therefore, you need to have a concept of yourself that is balanced, honest, positive, and healthy.

A Healthy Self-image

This is one of the concepts that has a huge impact on the way we enjoy life on a day-to-day basis. Somehow, the concept we have about ourselves affects so many of our attitudes, actions, and reactions, and even our relationships, as we confront the challenges of everyday life. This theme has to do with how we consider and accept ourselves in our physical appearance, on an intellectual level, in our emotions, and in how we relate to others. The concept we have about ourselves also will determine how we see others. In my years of counseling, this has been one of the major issues affecting a person on a deep level.

What do I mean by a healthy self-image? I define "healthy self-image" as the balanced, rational, truthful, positive, and modest concept of myself, which, in turn, will give me a sense of dignity, self-respect, and acceptance. It is easy to say these words, but in reality, more than 95 percent of individuals struggle with a good concept of themselves. It is so simplistic to suggest that a person "just needs to be positive about himself or herself." These struggles, in many cases, have become an agonizing battle, one that so many lose. I would like to make an analysis of this subject and provide some practical tools that I believe can help us overcome some of the pain and defeat in our lives.

It is interesting, Paul, in Romans 12:3, states the following: "For by the grace given me I say to every one of you: Do not think of yourself more highly than you ought, but rather think of yourself with sober judgment, in accordance with the measure of faith God has given you." What happens when you think more of yourself than is true? That is called pride and arrogance, and you well know that a proud person is disliked very easily. That is why someone said, "There is a sickness that makes everybody else fill bad, except for the one who has it." That is pride. Some people have sour memories of a relative or a friend who made a fool of himself or herself because of that stubborn pride.

On the other hand, when someone has a lower concept of himself than is true, we call that inferiority complex, and in this competitive world, you are not going to succeed if you have that problem. Someone looking at a person with a low concept of himself would like to shake that person and say, "React! Don't waste your life! You are worth much more than what you think." Others, with feelings of disgust, just ignore that person. Therefore, it is crucial to have a good, sober, and realistic concept of yourself to make the most of your life.

How is self-image established?

There are many factors that affect our self-esteem. One of them is plain and simply our temperament. Some are born with a tendency to be aggressive, optimistic go-getters, yet others have a natural tendency to be more passive, introverted, and negative. But this is only one reason; there are other factors as well.

All of us have been affected by memories—in some cases, very positive and edifying, but in many cases, very painful and negative experiences, and in other cases, even traumatic. I bet you have a series of stories to tell in regards to these experiences, some of them as far as you can remember.

There is an added ingredient to these memories, and that is our tendency to accept and remember more the negative ones than the positive ones. And on top of that, people who

53

surround us are more prone to pinpoint our mistakes and defects than our virtues and victories, in general.

The past has left scars, wounds, and issues in our lives that haven't been resolved yet. Some people need a couple of drinks before they can become more extroverted. The fact is that fear, anxiety, and insecurity invade a person, and some feel frozen or paralyzed from the things they would really like to do. Some have been controlled so much by these fears (phobias) that, in some cases, it has developed into more serious problems, such as depression, other mental illnesses, or panic attacks.

The present is overwhelming for people with a low self-esteem because this world is becoming more and more competitive and more demanding. Every day, the numbers are increasing of the people who need some type of medication to control their depression, anxiety, or fears.

I have been observing the way our society functions and how people are valued, especially by the media, which, in turn, become role models. As a result of that observation, I have concluded that our society, in general, follows these parameters:

- **Superficiality**: Physical appearance is of huge importance! For some, "appearance is all." Therefore, you pay careful attention to everything that has to do with this realm: weight, height (you have to be at least 5' 7" to participate in a beauty contest), brand name, style, where you buy things, how much they cost, who else is wearing those things, and so on.
- **Competitiveness**: You have to be number one. There is no room for losers. Some people have become so obsessed with this concept that they cannot cope with defeat. People try so hard to be better than others, or at least to keep up with others. They depend so much on what others may say.

- **Temporal and immediate gratification**: People are concerned about the present and pay little or no attention to the future; eternity is something you think about only when someone close to you dies.
- **Idealistic expectations**: Some have to be in such a rigid weight scale, or they will be terrified. One example of this is the number of people suffering from anorexia nervosa and some even dying for this cause.

As I was pondering this many years ago, I said to myself, "This is crazy! I don't want to subject myself to this kind of value system. I want to believe that there must be another way to establish a different system." So I did, and I have put it into practice ever since. I have used it in my counseling experience and during conferences for youths and adults. It has given me some good and satisfying experiences, and I would like to share with you the concepts.

Here is a different proposal that I believe goes along with common sense and is sustained by logical reasons, but most of all, with Christian principles.

- The first parameter, in opposition to superficiality, has to be **deeper and coherent**. We would relegate appearance to a second level and emphasize personal values and convictions as a better parameter to evaluate a person. We will pay more attention to the **virtues** of a person than the impressiveness of physical appearance. **The inside of a person is more valuable than the outer appearance**.
- In contrast to the second parameter of competitiveness, we will emphasize that we don't need to compete with others, our value doesn't depend on being superior or inferior to others, but we are grateful just to be who we are, and in anything we want to improve,

it would be for the glory of God. The results will be left to the Lord. But we will strive to do our best and be satisfied with that. **Individual worth without comparing ourselves with others is important.**

- To counter the parameter of just living for the day, we need to realize that what we do today affects our immediate future and, most of all, our eternity. **Eternity** should be the perspective we maintain in our everyday decisions.
- Against idealism, we need to be practical (pragmatic). That means we need to accept reality as it is, even if it is painful, instead of playing games with our minds and fantasizing about what is not going to happen. Mental health is defined as: to be relatively free from anxiety and in touch with reality. Idealistic people in terms of self-image have made the concept of being normal so narrow.

Let's take, as an example, our weight. We need to use common sense to realize that normal weight is a broader concept than ideal weight. You know how many people, especially women, become obsessed with this issue, bringing painful consequences to the individual and to the family. There are men caught in this tragedy also. Many of them are demanding their spouses or daughters conform to this idealistic expectation. It is so sad and sick! Yes, most of us would like a change here and there, but we need to accept our reality with a sound mind and with gratitude. Enough is enough! God is pleased with our physical appearance and accepts us just the way we are. He loves us, and we are very special to Him.

Following, I would like to share some reasons why our worth is very special. If you apply the parameters above, you will recognize that they are on agreement with those standards.

We are created in the image and likeness of God. We know this from Genesis 1:26-27, but what does it mean to be created in the image and likeness of God? God is Spirit, and we are flesh and bones. Also, God is invisible, and we are material beings, so how can we be His image and likeness?

Let me suggest that we are God's likeness and image in the following ways:

- Personhood: We are persons like God. A person is defined as the entity that has intellect, will, emotions, and understanding of good and evil. Those are characteristics of God, but also are characteristics of every human being. Everyone is born with these characteristics. We cannot compare ourselves with God because He is perfect in all, but at the same time, it is undeniable that all humans have these characteristics of personhood. Do you realize how special every single person is because of this? It is amazing to see how Satan, the world, and the flesh try to damage or attack those areas of our personality. We hear so many expressions to insult our intellect. People try to manipulate and control our will. We are wounded so many times in our emotions. And now more than ever, this world is trying to destroy our knowledge of good and evil by saying that there is not absolute truth. We need to stand and defend our personhood so that we won't be dragged by the current of this world. Do you realize that the understanding of our personality is a big part of our self-esteem? We need to start pondering and respecting each attribute of personhood. The more I think what it means to have my own will and my personal emotions, that I am an intelligent being and my own conscience, the more I become aware of the value of my individuality and personality. That also provokes a sense of self-respect and dignity. People will perceive somehow the respect you have for yourself. It will become a part of your subconscious.

- We are also God's image and likeness in that we have eternity in us, and all human beings possess this quality, whether it would be for eternal damnation or for eternal glory.

- We have a spiritual dimension, where God can communicate with us from His Spirit to our spirit. This is the most valuable characteristic. Jesus said, "What good will it be for a man if he gains the whole world, yet forfeits his soul? Or what can a man give in exchange for his soul?" (Matthew 16:26).

- We also have creativity. Of course, we cannot create from nothing; only God can do that. But we can create things from what we have. I am astonished at the advances in technology!

Another characteristic that helps us to have a positive self-image is the fact that **all human beings are original and unique.** There is no other person like you in all this world, and there has never been one like you! Just to prove it, no one else has your same fingerprints, or ears, and in the area of personality, you are you, period!

Your experiences in life are only yours. It is interesting that you can buy copies of the Mona Lisa by Leonardo da Vinci for a few dollars, but you cannot even buy the original painting. If it became for sale, it is worth millions of dollars. What is original is much more valuable than copies, and you are an original creation from God! Why, then, do we try to be copycats of others? Go figure!

Every human being has capacities and abilities to do something constructive in this world. The idea of being useless is a lie! We may not be talented for many things, but for sure, we have some abilities and capacities to do something meaningful.

This next concept applies only to God's people, but everyone, without exception, is invited to join in. Let me illustrate that concept with the following anecdote: There were six bottles of a special wine from the 1800s that were being auctioned off in Paris. A Japanese businessman decided to pay one hundred U.S. dollars for each bottle. If you wanted to have one of those bottles, I assume you would have to pay at least one hundred U.S. dollars for each bottle. You see, when someone paid that price for those bottles, that increased the value of those bottles of wine from then on.

If we apply that concept to you, where God paid for you the price of the life and the blood of His only Son, Jesus Christ, from that moment on, you became priceless! It is not pride; it is not arrogance. It is the truth! **The value of redemption! How can I consider myself of little value when God has already invested so much in me?**

When you are hurt by others, it seems like your self-image is the first thing to receive the blow. Having a good self-image does not mean that you don't get hurt anymore, but that you can recover fast, knowing who you really are. My suggestion for you is to meditate on these arguments for a good self-image until they become clear in your mind as your personal convictions—if you agree, of course!

The struggle will continue, but we can experience many more victories every single day. The truth sets us free.

UNDEALT WITH GUILT

> Blessed is he whose transgressions are forgiven, whose sins are covered.
>
> Psalm 32:1

Many of us have committed terrible mistakes (sins) in our lifetime, causing immeasurable damage to others, especially to loved ones and others around us, besides the great damage caused to ourselves. Or we may have done something that we know is really bad, but are scared to death to bring it out into the open, so we hide that sin to the best of our ability. We try our best to continue with life as normally as possible, while no one knows what our true story is.

If it were up to us, we would not let it come to light until we die. The fear of being discovered or being found out plagues our minds, and we cannot really rest or escape those shadows that go with us wherever we go. It is possible also that some of us are thinking, *I have gone too far, and there is no hope for me*, or, *If I were to open my mouth and tell someone what has been happening in my life or what I have done, I could not face the consequences; therefore, I'd rather keep the secret a little longer, even though this is killing me inside.*

Does it sound familiar to you? Does it make you feel uncomfortable right now as you read this part of this book?

I wish there were easy answers for these types of questions, but I would be a fool to try to answer in a simplistic way. Things are very complicated at times, and we cannot stop the law of cause and effect. So let me share some thoughts with you, and I hope and pray that God will give you some light and hope to start dealing with these complicated issues of hidden sins and the misery of guilt and shame that comes along.

- What you have done will come to light sooner or later. When that happens, you don't have any control over the results and consequences. Therefore, it is better to voluntarily assume your responsibilities and come clean, and expect some bad consequences, but you may have a little control over some things.

- People, in general, will be more merciful and understanding if you confess voluntarily, but there will be more anger and less mercy and understanding if you are caught in your own sin.
- When you are caught in your sin, there is the possibility that you don't truly repent. You may become just an arrogant person who is not sorry for the wrong you have done, but you are only sorry that you were caught (I'm *sorry* for the emphasis on and repetition of this word).
- When you let time go by without confronting you faults, most of the time, you keep falling into the same sin more and more, or start falling into other areas, too. Also, some situations become more complicated when you don't deal with your problems soon enough. Sometimes you may want to react when it is too late.
- When you face your sin and determine to open up, then faster and better restoration is available for you. More tools and help can be taken advantage of if you decide to come clean.
- Think of the prodigal son. God is waiting for you with His arms open wide. He is waiting for you to come back so He can show you His grace and mercy. God NEVER rejects someone who comes humbly and repentantly to Him. He may extend His grace to other people on your behalf, also.
- If you keep a rebellious attitude, then you are inviting more trouble for yourself, and God's discipline may be stronger than what you think. God cannot stand rebellion and arrogance.
- Bear in mind that some consequences for your actions do not occur because God is "mad" at you, but because there is a law that you will reap what you have sown.

- It is wiser and better to throw yourself in the merciful hands of God than to receive the uncontrolled consequences and reactions of those around you.

My personal recommendation is that you find a strong Christian friend or a pastor, and tell him or her what is happening in your life, then go from there, but first confess your sins to God and repent of them.

There is no better counsel than the Word of God, so let me share some passages for your help and comfort.

The sacrifices of God are a broken spirit; a broken and contrite heart, O God, you will not despise.

Psalm 51:17

"Come now, let us reason together," says the Lord. "Though your sins are like scarlet, they shall be as white as snow; though they are red as crimson, they shall be like wool."

Isaiah 1:18

Therefore confess your sins to each other and pray for each other so that you may be healed. The prayer of a righteous man is powerful and effective.

James 5:16

If we confess our sins, he is faithful and just and will forgive us our sins and purify us from all unrighteousness.

1 John 1:9

Please read Psalm 51 on your own. You will be blessed by it. King David wrote it after he fell in adultery, murder, and deceit. After he was confronted about his faults and he humbly accepted and confessed them, then his restoration process began.

A PERVASIVE, HABITUAL SIN

> Jesus replied: "I tell you the truth, everyone who sins is a slave to sin." . . . "So if the Son sets you free, you will be free indeed."
>
> John 8:34, 36

I don't know if there is more pain, frustration, shame, guilt, sense of defeat, and even sense of hopelessness than with the inability to shake off a certain sin that has enslaved a Christian. This is what we will call a "habitual sin" — something you have been struggling with for a while, you have asked for forgiveness for many times, and have pleaded for transformation from, but it seems that nothing is working successfully. Many questions and doubts arise within you. Is there any hope?

These bad habits are stronger than your desire and will to change. You may be wondering, *Why is it that God does not answer my prayer?*

This is a very touchy and complicated subject to deal with. I'm not going to say that I can deal with this in a satisfactory way, especially as I'm trying to deal with so many issues in this book. The thoughts that I'm going to share with you are some basic principles that can be applied in different circumstances, and, Lord willing, there will be a door that gives you hope, knowing that God is in the business of restoring the whole person. In the future, if the Lord wills, I'll be writing a book concentrated only on this topic.

What are we talking about when we say "habitual sins"? These are sins that we are controlled by. It is too easy to fall into them. They are committed repeatedly or frequently. It is your weak area, where you are the most vulnerable. Let me give a brief list of them, but these are not all of them. A person can have one or more of these sins controlling his life:

- Lying: changing the truth, exaggerating the facts, telling only certain parts of the truth, according to your convenience, hiding the truth.
- Stealing: little things or big things. Taking without permission what does not belong to you.
- Lust: looking to someone with desire who is not your husband or wife.
- Lasciviousness or sensuality: acting in a seductive way or dressing in a way that provokes or entices others who are not your spouse with desire toward you.
- Pornography: purchasing or watching sexual images, including nudity for personal gratification, whether pictures, movies, magazines, the Internet, or other means.
- Adultery: sexual experiences outside of marriage.
- Fornication: sexual experiences before getting married.
- Bitterness and resentment: maintaining anger, disgust, and resentment toward anyone without dealing with the offender or coming to a place of forgiveness.
- Gluttony: compulsive eating, eating too much, including bulimia.
- Worry and anxiety: being overly concerned about something or the future with a lack of faith and with fear.
- Drunkenness: regular use of alcohol, whether monthly, weekly, or daily.
- Profanity: the use of vulgar and offensive language in regular conversation or jokes, or when you are mad at someone. This includes swearing.

This list is only an example of the many habitual sins that plague our society and even our homes and churches.

Many of these bad habits usually are the symptoms of deeper and bigger problems. They do need personal and diligent attention, but they do have a common root. **There is usually a lie or lies that control that behavior.** Take any one of the examples on this list, and see what the lie is behind it. Let me take one of them: Lasciviousness or sensuality. Let's look at some lies that are behind this sin:

- "If others are looking at me in a sinful way, that is their problem, not mine. I'm dressing 'innocently.'"
- "Come on! This is only a fashion! Everybody else is doing it! I don't see anything wrong with that. We should not go to extremes; let's be real!"
- "I'm just trying to be attractive; I don't see anything wrong with that."

Let me ask you these questions:

- Are you attracting others to you as a whole person or only as an object of lust?
- Do you think that God is being honored by the way you dress?
- Isn't provoking someone to fall something that you become responsible for?
- Did you know that God expects you to dress with modesty (1 Timothy 2:9)?

The Word of God says, "And you will know the truth, and the truth will set you free." So how can you experience freedom from habitual sins?

- First, you need to realize you cannot overcome by your own strength. You need someone more powerful than you, and that is God Himself.
- God wants to set you free. He came so that we may be free.
- He already paid for your sin or sins; now He wants for you to walk in victory.
- Do you really want to be free and for God to help you? I have found in my experience as a counselor that many just WISH to be free; they just want the "magic formula," but they do not REALLY WANT to be free because if they are demanded to do something radical, they are not willing to. I was helping a gentleman addicted to alcohol, and he was losing his family for this reason. I asked him if he was willing to give up his "buddies" with whom he got drunk every week and sometimes every day. He confessed to me that he was not willing to do that, so he continued with his addiction in spite of the consequences he was already facing.
- Jesus said, "Apart from me you can do nothing." If you want to be free, you will need to desire God with all your heart and to surrender your life to Christ. I have seen that there is no addiction that you can't overcome with God's help, but without your total surrender to Him, it won't work, or it won't last.
- Many addictions are connected to other areas of your life. Do you want for God to deal with all areas of your life, or just with "this problem"? God is absolute; He wants to be in control of all your life for your own sake because you have already demonstrated what your life is like under your own administration.
- You will need the fellowship of other Christians for encouragement and accountability, and on a regular basis. There is something special and powerful when

we are connected with others who are like-minded. This can really make a difference in your life as you face struggles.

- Spiritual exercises are a must if you expect victory in your life. I will discuss that in the third part of this book. There are tools that God has put in your hands. God does not ask you to do something that He will not enable and give you the tools to do.

My hope is that as you have reflected on this issue, you have made a choice that you are going to pursue victory in your life, and nobody is going to deter or discourage you until you experience the freedom available in Christ.

Submit yourselves, then, to God. Resist the devil, and he will flee from you.

James 4:7

From personal experience, I've learned the secret of victory is to confess our sins, seek the Lord with all our hearts, and surrender completely to Him. I hope you do the same.

I would like to recommend a really good book on this subject: *The Bondage Breaker*, by Dr. Neil T. Anderson.

THE POISON OF BITTERNESS

Get rid of all bitterness, rage and anger, brawling and slander, along with every form of malice.

Ephesians 4:31

Man accused of killing wife, self was served divorce papers. (December 27, 2008)[1]
Man gets five years for driving into his mother in parking lot. (August 29, 2008)[2]

Charles Joseph Whitman (June 24, 1941-August 1, 1966) was a student at the University of Texas at Austin who killed 14 people and wounded 32 others as part of a shooting rampage on and around the campus of the University of Texas at Austin. Three were killed inside the university's tower and ten killed from the observation deck of the university's 32-story administrative building on August 1, 1966; one died a week later from her wounds. He did this shortly after murdering his wife and mother at their homes.[3]

The Virginia Tech massacre was a school shooting consisting of two separate attacks approximately two hours apart on April 16, 2007, that took place on the campus of Virginia Polytechnic Institute and State University (Virginia Tech) in Blacksburg, Virginia, United States. The perpetrator, Seung-Hui Cho, killed 32 people and wounded many others before committing suicide.[4]

I don't know if I have seen something more powerful and damaging as bitterness. I have seen good, wholesome people become low, nasty, and revengeful. I have seen marriages destroyed by this plague. I have seen churches divided and devastated by this sin. I have seen children hating their parents because of it. I have seen best friends become worst enemies.

This sin of bitterness disfigures a person, divides, consumes, destroys, enslaves, and even kills.

I'm afraid we don't pay enough attention to this problem in our lives and in the lives of those around us, and when we deal with this problem, we treat it in such a superficial way. We even dare to use expressions like, "Just let it go," as if it were a garment we can just take off. We underestimate the destructive power of this sin and the depth of its roots.

This sin is similar to pride in that many times, it is hard to realize you have it because it is so easy to deny it or to hide it. It can be undetected or overlooked, when in reality, it can be a time bomb.

What is behind that bitterness, resentment, and anger? It is a hurt that hasn't been healed or treated; therefore, it is festering inside. We may say that bitterness is that emotion of resentment and anger when we have been hurt by someone intentionally or unintentionally, or even if it's imagined.

There are different ways that we can detect bitterness in someone, and I would venture to say that there are at least three types of bitter people:

- The typical "victim" is always negative, pessimistic, hypersensitive, resentful, with a strong persecution complex, and depressive.
- The cold and distant person is insecure, mistrusting, quiet, uninvolved in the life of others, and rejects and dislikes others very easily.
- The hostile and offensive person is hypercritical, finds defects in everyone, doesn't agree with many, puts down people frequently, is rude and a bully, and can be very abusive and intimidating.

Bitterness is also contagious because a bitter person will predispose others to resent the person he resents. That is why Scripture in Hebrews 12:15 says: "See to it that no one misses the grace of God and that no bitter root grows up to cause trouble and defile many."

Bitterness not only grows like a weed if unattended, but also becomes addictive. A person can become literally engulfed in and controlled by it. In my years of experience, I have discovered many cases of deep depression rooted in bitterness; in fact, it has been so encouraging to see depressed people become positive and normal after dealing with their bitterness.

There will be the tendency to identify others having this problem, but let me assure you that many of you who are reading this book are struggling right now with this problem of bitterness, anger, and resentment. So what can be done in order to become free of this malady?

The first thing to do is to recognize that you have this problem. You may need to ask God to reveal this sin to you through His Holy Spirit. Psalm 139:23-24 says: "Search me, O God, and know my heart; test me and know my anxious thoughts. See if there is any offensive way in me, and lead me in the way everlasting."

If you realize that you have this problem, then you need to confess it to God and repent so that you will be free.

Now, you need to forgive those who have hurt you. In many cases, this is not easy, so let me walk you through this process of forgiving others. You need to let God help you with this. You are going to need His love and grace to overcome this bondage.

Jesus taught us that whatever we bind on earth will be bound in heaven, and whatever we loose on earth will be loosed in heaven (see Matthew 16:19). Let me give you this illustration: If you offend one of my children, you are in trouble with me, but if you apologize to my child who was offended, then it is resolved with me also. So, whatever we do to anyone affects God directly.

In the Lord's Prayer, we also repeat, ". . . forgive us our trespasses, as we forgive those who trespass against us." This implies that we forgive others as God forgives us.

Let me explain this process of forgiveness:

What is forgiveness?

- Forgiveness is an act of the will. Sometimes your emotions are going to be against what you want to do. You may be reasoning and feeling something is not fair, or feeling like a hypocrite because you don't really want to forgive. You need to make up your mind. Do you really want to be free, or do you want to keep yourself in the prison of bitterness?

- Forgiveness is a commandment from God. IT IS NOT OPTIONAL FOR THE BELIEVER. If you are God's child, there is no other option. You have no idea the freedom and the many blessings you will have because of this act of obedience. Trust me; I have been there!
- Forgiveness is willingly living with the consequences of someone else's faults. There are some damages that will last your lifetime, and you need to cope with them. There is no other way, except through forgiveness. Then you will be able to move on with your life and let God be glorified in you.
- Forgiveness is canceling ALL debts. From now on, the person that offended you does not owe you anything! It will seem contradictory and unfair, but you will discover that there is an abundance of life and peace waiting for you.
- Forgiveness is setting the offender free. That is when you can say, "I have let the offender go, instead of keeping him or her tied up to my life." You will be liberating two people: him or her and yourself.
- Forgiveness is deciding not to bring a fault against that person again. There is no room for recriminations against that person in the future on account of what you have already forgiven.

What is NOT forgiveness?

- Forgetting. Especially if the wound was deep, there is no way you will forget. Don't even try to forget, but try to heal the wound. When a wound is healed, you won't remember as often, and you may even forget for long periods of time.

- Excusing or minimizing is a big mistake because if we are going to forgive something, it is better to be honest with ourselves, and recognize what it is exactly that we are forgiving. You can excuse anything that is insignificant, like someone coming five minutes late to an appointment, but you cannot excuse a big offense; it won't help you at all.
- Justifying or reasoning away is another mistake we can commit in this area. Maybe we think that in that way, we are being very merciful and understanding. But it won't bring real healing and peace. Everybody needs to be accountable for his own actions. I have a personal expression on this matter: "When somebody hurts me, I don't excuse; I only forgive."

Why forgive?

- For my own sake. It may sound selfish, but in reality, it is not. God wants my freedom. If I don't forgive, I keep hurting myself after all the pain I have already experienced. This is a smart move on my part. There is a self-deception to think that I'm punishing the other person when, in reality, it is me who I'm punishing.
- For the glory of God. In humble obedience, I submit to His will, and I don't want to be found in rebellion and defiance of the One who loves me so much! I not only want to obey Him, but I want to follow His example.
- For the sake of the offender. Where would this world be if everybody was charged for what everyone has done? Where would I be if I had to pay for each one of my wrong actions? I need mercy! And so does the other person!
- For the sake of His kingdom. If I get rid of bitterness and learn to forgive others, then maybe many

will realize that Christianity, indeed, is the better way to live, and maybe others would be interested in knowing who the One is who has set us free from so much hatred and misery.

The steps of forgiveness:

- Identify and acknowledge the offense and the offender. Do not generalize; call the person and the offense by name, instead of making this special moment so vague and meaningless.
- Evaluate the damage. Once and for all, take a last look at the real damage that was caused to you by the other person so you won't forgive a partial debt, but a complete one.
- Express the offense and the damage and the pain to God because He is going to take that burden from you and heal your wounds. Let God treat you completely.
- Declare the forgiveness. Express to God that willingly and voluntarily you choose to forgive the offender.
- Ask for blessings on the offender. This is a very difficult step to take. Don't trust in your emotions; just do it as an act of obedience. You will see the results later.
- Confess YOUR sins of bitterness, hatred, and resentment. Remember that hating someone is the same as committing murder, according to God, so please don't excuse yourself, and accept your own responsibility.
- Accept God's forgiveness. He has forgiven you and will set you free. Thank God for what He is doing and for what He will do in your life.
- Express the forgiveness to the offender when possible. It may be face to face, by phone, through a letter, and so on.

- Be willing to be of service to the offender. This is another tough task to do, especially the first time, but once you have done it, the next time it will be easier.

In some cases, you may want the support of having a strong Christian with you as you go through this process of forgiveness. I pray that God will give you the strength and courage to obey Him.

The late Dr. Adrian Rogers, who has been a great instrument of God in my life, used to say, "Justice is giving what somebody deserves, mercy is not giving what the other deserves, and grace is giving what the other doesn't deserve." I have been trying to apply this concept in my life, and the joy I have experienced because of it has been amazing and rewarding.

1. Headline appeared in *The Argus Leader*, a local newspaper in Sioux Falls, South Dakota.
2. Ibid.
3. Story taken from Wikipedia, the Free Encyclopedia.
4. Ibid.

THE COMFORT OF MEDIOCRITY

So, because you are lukewarm—neither hot nor cold—I am about to spit you out of my mouth.
Revelation 3:16

How comfortable to feel comfortable! There is such a coziness about being comfortable. I'm imagining a wintry day when the temperature outside is below zero. I'm lying on a couch with a warm blanket and a soft pillow under my head, watching a very interesting movie, and somebody rings the bell. I know I have to get up and answer the door. *It better be something important*, I think, because I didn't want to get up in the first place!

There is nothing wrong with my wanting to be comfortable, but what if I needed to go to work or I needed to take the kids to school—should I choose my comfort over my responsibility? Of course not! Common sense dictates that I need to become uncomfortable for the sake of my responsibilities. If I don't do what is responsible, I may even be called "a lazy bum."

The tragedy in the lives of many people is that they have become so attached to their comfort zone that they don't want to even think that God is expecting us to bear much fruit to glorify Him and demonstrate that we are truly His disciples. "This is to my Father's glory, that you bear much fruit, showing yourselves to be my disciples" (John 15:8).

We can become so comfortable that we become lazy, insensitive, and careless.

There are some areas where we can become mediocre and even useless. They include:

- Physical personal care. We are the temple of the Holy Spirit; therefore, we need to treat our bodies with responsibility and care. We should rest what is necessary, feed ourselves in a healthy way, keep ourselves physically clean, dress up with modesty. We are stewards of our bodies; therefore, we must protect them.

- Work/studies. We need to work or study (if you are a student) with responsibility as unto the Lord to bring Him honor and give a good testimony to those around you in your field of work or to those around you at school.

- Family relationships. We need to remember that we are responsible for building up everyone around us at home. It is so easy to tear them down; any fool can do that. But it demands diligence and wisdom to build others up. We must spend time with our families and not waste the few years that we are with them. We must build good, fun memories at home because we have no idea of the impact those memories will have on an individual as he or she moves on with his or her life.

- Hobbies/sports/entertainment. Have fun, and enjoy life! Do things that are entertaining, enjoyable, constructive, and relaxing. Those around you will enjoy being with you if you know how to enjoy life. Don't make home a boring place to be.
- Personal devotions/spiritual walk. Build good habits because they will build your character. It does demand discipline, and for most of us, it does not come easy, but the rewards are for this life and for eternity to come. Don't take shortcuts. Consistency will pay off; you will enjoy a good reputation. Just remember what somebody has said: "Reputation is what people think of you, but character is what God thinks of you."
- Church/fellowship. Don't neglect the fellowship with other believers. Many of them will be with you in your times of need and trials. They will be a source of encouragement and accountability. Enjoy corporate worship and learning or teaching the Word of God. God's family will last for eternity.
- Service. There are so many blessings for those who have chosen to dedicate their lives to serving others. In most cases, there are more blessings for the one who serves than the one who is served. There is a thrill in sharing your talent, time, and resources with others. Sometimes it is hard to put into words the joy a person experiences through service.

- Generosity. This is clearly a paradox; the more you give away, the more you get. I'm not talking about material rewards, even though sometimes that happens also. Don't give with the intention of receiving material things back; learn to give just for the pleasure of simply giving.
- Witness. There is so much bad news every day on the radio, on TV, and in the newspaper, as well as negative conversations. Bring light and good news to a society that is growing in thick darkness as evil grows day to day. People are dying without hope. Are we going to keep silent just because it is uncomfortable and a little risky? Are not people more important than our fear? Please ask God to help you in this.
- Leadership. Bottom line: Leadership is influence. Ask yourself, "Am I a good influence on others?" And if you are a parent, are you a good influence on those at home? You cannot avoid this; you are an influence anyway!

I have called it "the survival mode" when someone has no ambition for life; doesn't want to grow emotionally, intellectually, or spiritually; doesn't want any challenges; and does not want to dream again, but only wants to vegetate. If you want to experience abundant life, you need to leave that "mode." Make your life count!

A business without a vision is doomed to failure. In fact, any organization without a vision will stop growing and, in many cases, collapse. In the same way, if we don't have a vision for our lives, we will be just surviving or vegetating, and that is not a real life, not the life God has called us to live. With no vision, there are no goals, and with no goals, there is nothing to measure your life by, whether you are progressing or not.

Be very careful, then, how you live—not as unwise
but as wise, making the most of every opportunity,
because the days are evil.

Ephesians 5:15-16

Teach us to number our days aright, that we may gain
a heart of wisdom.

Psalm 90:12

THE LOVE OF MONEY

For the love of money is a root of all kinds of evil.
Some people, eager for money, have wandered from
the faith and pierced themselves with many griefs.

1 Timothy 6:10

Is wealth evil? Absolutely not! The problem is not being
wealthy or poor, but our attitude and affection toward money
and wealth. It is the **love of money** that is the problem. In
order to make my point on this matter, let me share with you
two other verses from the Bible:

No servant can serve two masters. Either he will hate
the one and love the other, or he will be devoted to
the one and despise the other. You cannot serve both
God and Money.

Luke 16:13

Whoever loves money never has money enough;
whoever loves wealth is never satisfied with his
income. This too is meaningless.

Ecclesiastes 5:10

A successful businessman due to his work had to travel to
many countries, and he would make sure that in every single

trip, he would bring a nice souvenir to his only daughter, whom he loved so much. One day as he presented another gift to his daughter, she told him, "Daddy, I really like all the gifts you bring to me from your trips, but I don't want them anymore." Her Father, in astonishment, asked her, "What is it that you want, then?" His daughter replied, "I just want to spend some time with you because I hardly see you. You are not around here too much."

It saddens me to see over and over again how many parents have been trapped in their pursuit of fortune, trying to give a better future to their loved ones, but damaging their most important relationships in the process.

There are some reasons that lead many into this pitfall. Let me enumerate some of them:

- I want to give to them what I didn't have when I was growing up.
- I just want to build a safe nest for the future because who knows how long I'll be around?
- This is the American Dream, and I am planning on fulfilling it.
- I just want to be a millionaire, I'm sorry, a billionaire.
- This world is for winners, not losers, and for sure, I don't want to be a loser.
- I want to have what the Joneses have.
- We need to be ambitious in life, right?
- The wealthiest people in the Bible were godly people, like Abraham, Job, King Solomon, Joseph, and so on.
- What I do with my life is my business. Mind your own business!

Let me say it again: There is nothing wrong with having wealth, and I do agree that to a point, it is good to be ambitious, there is nothing wrong with trying to prosper, and, yes, many godly people in the Bible were very rich because God blessed them. However, I want to point out one word from Luke 16:13, and that word is "MASTER." I once heard somebody say, "The problem is not if you have money, but if money has you."

Do you have money or wealth that you manage as a tool that God has given you to bless your family and the advancement of His kingdom here on earth? Or is it for your own personal interests and desires? Is the wealth you have to glorify God and invest in things for eternity? Or is it to invest only in yourself? Has money become your master? What do you think those who know you best would think about you on this matter? Who is the real owner, God or you?

The chaotic economy in our current world should be a wake-up call for all of us to understand that greed is an evil that causes so much suffering and injustice. Many people are recognizing that the root problem in our financial world is the love of money, known also as greed.

If we want to enjoy life, we need to get rid of this love of money. I do realize this will be a very challenging subject for some, but let me assure you that there is a liberating experience for those who have chosen to become God's administrators, rather than owners, of wealth.

There is another side to this issue of money, and that has to do more with those of us who don't have too much.

This society has become too much of a consumer world. We want to have almost everything that is being advertised. Again, there is nothing wrong with wanting to get something that would make our lives more comfortable and useful.

Right now, I'm using my computer instead of a typewriter. Could you imagine me trying to write this book in the old style? Then, what is the problem? The problem is that many of us are living beyond our means, and some others are piling up things at home that will never be used, or will maybe be used once. That is called waste!

For those who can afford things and are piling stuff just for the sake of having it, this is not good stewardship. For some, this problem of getting things is becoming a bad habit that is called compulsive shopping. I believe God wants to deliver us from this compulsive behavior, whatever the root cause may be. I had to deal with this issue in my own life a few years ago.

On the other issue of living beyond our means, the easy credit available in our modern world is making things worse. With the ability to purchase anything on credit, many are buying whatever they wish, and later on they are realizing that paying back is not as easy as expected.

I have been a firsthand witness of the destruction of many lives and many homes because of this ambition to live and enjoy life with material things way over our financial capacity to pay. We need to wake up to our reality and adjust our lives to the facts of our income. If we want to see better days, we must evaluate our lifestyle seriously and determine if we need to repent and change. God, with His mercy and grace, is ready to restore us in this area of life also.

There are many Christian books that deal with the subject of finances. I recommend visiting a bookstore that sells this type of literature. Some churches and organizations even have ministries devoted to dealing with these issues.

PRIDE: THE UNDETECTED ENEMY

When pride comes, then comes disgrace, but with humility comes wisdom.

Proverbs 11:2

Pride goes before destruction, a haughty spirit before a fall.

Proverbs 16:18

The Lord detests all the proud of heart. Be sure of this: They will not go unpunished.

Proverbs 16:5

Webster's definition of pride: a) an unduly high opinion of oneself; exaggerated self-esteem; conceit b) haughty behavior resulting from this; arrogance.

On one occasion, I had a couple in my office wanting to resolve their marriage in crisis. Trying to have an idea of what was going on, I told them that I would be asking them different questions and that I was expecting their answers to be as honest as possible. Both of them agreed. One of the questions I asked was: What do you think are your worst defects that are causing damage to you marriage?

The wife was the one to answer first, and she said, "Well, I'm a resentful person, and when I'm hurt, I don't talk to him at all." Also, she said, "I spend too much time at my mom's house, neglecting some responsibilities at my own home," and she mentioned a couple more of her faults. Then I turned to the husband and asked the same question, to which he responded, "My fault is that I'm too good, yes, I am stupid because I am too good to a fault! Yes, sir, that is my fault!" His answer gave the understanding of what his major fault was: his pride!

Have you ever been in front of those funny mirrors that distort your image? I have, and it was very funny to see myself "in a different light." I was laughing a lot. Of course, my friends and family members who were looking at me in the mirror had an even better time watching me in that mirror!

Pride is a distorting mirror, except it is not funny. In fact, it is ugly. The consequences are immeasurable. Pride is an exaggerated view of yourself that deceives you into thinking that you are great or superior, when in reality, those around you are annoyed by your attitudes, some of them are mad at and disgusted with you, and some even feel pity for you. Of course, most won't tell you a word, and even some may smile at you, or they may act as if they were in agreement with you. What a sad picture!

When I'm saying "you," I also mean "me." To my shame, many times I have made a fool of myself, and I'm not free yet. There will be days when I may repeat the same mistake. I did use the pronoun "you" because I do want to challenge you, and I want to be direct.

Some of the symptoms of pride are:

- A refusal to look for and accept the counsel of others or their advice; an unwillingness to learn from others.
- An attitude that you can do without others; you are self-sufficient.
- People know you as a stubborn person.
- You get irritated when someone corrects you.
- You will not admit mistakes or faults and are always trying to justify yourself.
- You feel superior to others. You are always comparing yourself.
- You talk a lot about yourself. You crave people's recognition.
- You are usually on the defense.

Below, you will read some paragraphs that describe some of the effects and implications of pride, and why I have called pride "the undetected enemy."

- Pride damages your image. It does not make you look better, but it makes you look foolish and sometimes even ridiculous.
- Pride makes you blind to your own faults, which complicates your relationships with others because you are not able to correct what you don't see. Many times you are hurting others with your attitudes, words, and actions, but you are not able to perceive it.
- Pride makes you deaf to the counsel, suggestions, and guidance of others because you are self-sufficient, too smart and knowledgeable to pay attention to what they are saying, and you don't realize that there is wisdom in the counsel of many.
- Pride builds a wall around you and causes you to lose something extremely precious: the intimacy of loved ones and the closeness of true friends. People around you find it difficult to be close to you because you don't know how to open up or to drop your guard, relax, and be transparent.
- Pride makes you a slave. You make for yourself your own little world because it becomes very hard for you to share yourself with others on a deeper level. You may just keep giving excuses by saying that is just the way you are, and not give yourself a chance to change and grow.
- Most of all, pride damages your relationship with God because you are not able to see many of your sins; your conscience becomes harder and harder. God wants to do so many things in you and through you, but you are not allowing God to show you what He wants for your life and what He can do through you. You may perceive God as very distant from you, and that is right because God cannot stand pride and arrogance. If you want to come to Him, you must come in complete humility.

- Pride won't allow you to heal relationships because you cannot recognize your faults, and if you do, you may not be able to confess those faults and say, "I'm sorry!"
- Pride makes you feel like you don't need God much, or at all! It makes you too independent of others, thinking you don't need them.
- Pride populates hell because many will die thinking that they don't need a Savior.
- Pride will make you an ungrateful person. You may think everybody owes you, or you will take many things and people for granted.

As you can see, pride is very damaging to a person. It is an enemy that we need to try to keep as far as possible from us. It does creep in in subtle ways. There are so many forms of pride, and as I said earlier, sometimes it is hard to detect our own pride. We do need the help of others, but especially of the Holy Spirit, so we can become more and more sensitive to pride's presence in our lives, so we can deal with pride in a proper manner.

The antidote to pride is humility, and I'll be dealing specifically with that subject in Part III of this book.

Don't let pride rob you of the abundance of life God has for you. It is your choice.

LIVING IN THE PAST

Brothers, I do not consider myself yet to have taken hold of it. But one thing I do: Forgetting what is behind and straining toward what is ahead, I press on toward the goal to win the prize for which God has called me heavenward in Christ Jesus.

Philippians 3:13-14

Judas, after realizing what he had done, tried unsuccessfully to undo his treason by returning the thirty silver coins, but it was too late! The people who gave him the money did not care for him anymore, or about his remorse or whatever else he was feeling, so in the midst of his desperation and guilt, he went and hanged himself.

We all have something we regret from our past, but some have many more and greater regrets than others. How many of us wish there was a way to return to the past and make things right? In fact, some movies deal with this dream of being able to go back and change certain things that would give people a better present and future. Unfortunately, that is just science fiction; the reality of life hits us very hard.

As I ponder this, I realize that there are a few types of regrets: regrets about what we said, regrets about what we did, regrets about what we didn't do, regrets about what we didn't say, regrets about the hurts we experienced that were someone else's fault, and regrets about our circumstances.

"I'm so sorry!" "I didn't really mean it!" "Please forgive me!" are things I have said, or, I would like to say, but those words I have pronounced are already out of my mouth, and I can't take them back; it is too late! Sometimes we meant what we said, and what we said probably was the truth, but then we realized it was not prudent at all! Spoken words are so powerful, and they can be so destructive. When we see the results and the negative impact of those words, then it dawns on us, *I shouldn't have said that. I should have just shut my mouth!*

Many sad memories come to my mind as I recall my imprudent words, or words I said in a moment of anger, or just careless words that were not handled with wisdom or prudence, or a joke that offended someone.

I cannot undo the past. What can I do so those ghosts won't come to torment me anymore? I would like to suggest some steps:

- **Make restitution.** Talk to the person you have offended, and without giving an excuse, tell that person that you are sorry for what you have said. This is a very difficult thing to do, but I am confident that God will give you the strength you need, if you are willing to do everything you can to make things right. Just please, be honest, humble, and direct. The moment you try to justify what you have said, the other person will feel more offended, and it will be harder for him or her to forgive you. If you are not able to talk face to face, then do it by phone, or write that person a letter, or send an e-mail. Take advantage of this moment that you feel motivated and compelled. This is your right time!

- **Accept the past as a lesson for your present and future.** As it has been stated already, we cannot change the past; therefore, we need to accept it. If you have done any restitution, then you can move on with no more guilt, but make sure you take advantage of your past by learning lessons regarding what you should not do or what you should avoid. If guilt continues to haunt you, you need to realize that it does not come from God. If there is a situation where it is impossible to make restitution, then just ask God for forgiveness, and He will grant it to you immediately. Read this counsel from Scripture: "My dear brothers, take note of this: Everyone should be quick to listen, slow to speak and slow to become angry" (James 1:19).

- The late President Reagan said, "We don't negotiate with terrorists." I like that phrase! And I would like to use it in the following way: When haunted by memories of the past, remember that you have already been forgiven, and then ignore those thoughts; do not entertain them in your mind. **Do not negotiate with negative thoughts**, period!

The same principles apply to the other types of regrets. You must have heard the expression "It is better late than never." In the area of making things right, while you are alive and there is an opportunity to restore something, just do it. I know sometimes there is a sense of overwhelming fear, shame, or guilt, but you won't regret that you did something about it.

Is there a debt you never paid to someone, which has caused a distance between the two of you? Is there a promise you've never fulfilled? Is there a book or something you never returned? It there a clarification you never made? Is there a letter you never replied to? Is there something you were wrong about but never made the other person know? Is there a lie you need to confess? Is there an offense you need to apologize for?

I have found that for many people, it is easier to forgive others, but very difficult to forgive themselves. Some can be very merciful to others, but extremely hard on themselves. When God commanded us to love our neighbor as ourselves, it implies that you must love yourself.

When I have become extremely harsh with myself, I had to ask myself this question: If I was helping someone with the same problem that I have right now, how would I treat and react to that person? Then I would say to myself, "Do likewise for yourself." It is not easy! But it is the right thing to do. And I can't emphasize enough: Forgive yourself, accept your past, and accept yourself. You won't be free from your negative memories if you don't do that.

Forget the past, as it is recommended by the apostle Paul. Does he really mean to forget? Not in a literal sense because there is not a mechanism in our memory to erase our past or parts of our past, but we do have the capacity to put the past to the side and move on with the present and future, and when referring to our past, we would use it with positive intentions.

Look at the example of Paul. On many occasions, he used his past to explain something beneficial to others or to demonstrate how God's grace has worked in his life. So if we use our past as a springboard for the future or to bless someone, then it is correct to go back to our past, but if bringing the past back is to discourage, to feel guilty and miserable, then we need to put our past behind us.

PART III

WHAT YOU MUST HAVE TO BE SUCCESSFUL IN LIFE

How do you define "success"?

For many in our world, "success" is having reached a goal of obtaining a college degree, acquiring "enough" fortune, enjoying some popularity and fame, becoming part of the book *Guinness World Records*, becoming number one in a sport discipline, getting medals in the Olympics, being awarded the Nobel prize, obtaining a managing position in the corporate world, having a thriving business, and so on. Nobody can deny that this is success, and that is fine, to a certain point. The sad part is that these types of successes are the ONLY ones they are looking for, like if THIS WERE THE ONLY LIFE TO LIVE, but when you add ETERNITY to your life, then the perspective of success changes dramatically. In other words, THE CONCEPT AND CONVICTION YOU HAVE ABOUT YOUR OWN ETERNITY are going to powerfully and directly influence your definition of "success."

I submit to you that real success is having the approval of God. After everything is said and done, to hear God say to you in front of all His angels and in front of all creation,

"Well done, good and faithful servant." I think many people are waiting for too small of a recognition, namely from mere men, when you can get a much better recognition than that. I would challenge you to be a more ambitious person in regards to this.

Another way of measuring and defining success is at the end of our lives. What would those who know us think of the memories we have left with them? Will people who knew you well say, "He lived a life that is worth imitating," or would they say, "I don't want to be like him."

I don't like the idea of just living day to day without making a difference in the lives of others. We should make our lives count for something. Did you know that there is a relief and gladness when someone evil dies? I have heard literally this words "Thank goodness so-and-so is gone!"

If someone wrote an epitaph on your tombstone, what do you think it would say? I would like to ask you to do something: Why don't you take a piece of paper and try to write a sentence like an epitaph that would describe what your life was all about?

Another question that would help you put your life in perspective would be, What do you think God would say about you?

Now, let me ask you, What is the legacy you will leave for those you love and who are close to you?

As you can see, life is not an accident, but it is something we must take seriously. We cannot afford to leave it to chance, but intentionally and deliberately, we need to make intelligent choices.

In this part of this book, I will share with you some of the principles and choices we need to make in order to harvest a life with purpose and meaning. So please, enjoy this last part of the book.

A SOUND KNOWLEDGE OF GOD

The fear of the Lord is the beginning of wisdom, and knowledge of the Holy One is understanding.

Proverbs 9:10

The most important question you can ask in your life is, WHO IS GOD? Because the answer to that question will determine the type of relationship you have with Him and how you relate to Him. It also will affect the way you live. Of course, I'm not talking about some vague and intellectual idea about God, but true convictions or, in other words, what you *really* believe in your mind and in your heart.

To try to answer that question in a way is an impossible task because how can you define the infinite? How do you understand the incompressible? How do you describe the indescribable? On the other hand, God has decided to reveal things to us through the things He has made, through His Word, and through His Son, Jesus.

Thanks to those three revelations, we can have an adequate and comprehensible concept of God. It by no means implies that we can comprehend completely, but our grasp and understanding of God will lead us to a personal relationship with our Creator and will inspire us to live according to His pleasant and perfect will.

We do have the whole Bible to answer the question "Who is God?" and after theologians have spent all their lives studying it, they will realize that God is much more than what they can think or imagine. So please, allow me to share a very few limited ideas of who God is, and I expect to be faithful to His Word.

- God is almighty. It implies that God can do anything without limit, but He won't do anything against His

93

own nature. God cannot lie or sin in any shape or form.

- God is holy. That means God is pure and the sum of His entire moral attributes in perfection.
- God is perfect in all His ways; He is never wrong. Everything He does is perfect.
- God is good. God always has our best in mind, even though we don't understand at times, like a child when he is corrected by his parents.
- God is love. His love is unconditional and eternal. He is still waiting for those who reject, hate, and oppose Him. The highest expression of His love is that He gave His only begotten Son to die for us.
- God is merciful. He has compassion for us and doesn't want to pay us according to what we deserve.
- God is gracious. Not only does He have compassion for us, but He gives us good things we don't deserve. The greatest gift He has given us is His Son and, through Him, eternal life.
- God is wise. We can rely on His knowledge and wisdom. What He wants for me is better than what I want for myself. He knows all things; He knows the past and the future, so He is qualified to tell us what is better for us.
- God is omniscient. He knows everything, even the intentions of my heart and all the thoughts that go through my mind, not to mention what I say and do.
- God is eternal. God is not affected by time. Time was created for men; that is why for God, one day is like a thousand years, or a thousand years like a day.
- God is the Creator. He created all things, including us, and He is the sustainer of everything. All was created for Him and by Him.
- God is the only Savior. There is no salvation outside of God.

- God is omnipresent. He is everywhere; there is no place where His presence is not.
- God is immutable. That means He does not change. We can rest in the fact that God is what He says He is. He is constant and reliable.
- God is just. There is not impunity with God; if we don't come to His saving grace, we will have to face the justice of His hand.

This list is very limited and with little explanation. It's not enough to satisfy anyone, but I do challenge you to get into His Word and let Him guide you to all truth.

A good knowledge of God will transform your life and will produce in you a desire to worship Him, a love that grows deeper and deeper as you fellowship with Him, a hunger to know Him more intimately, a desire to serve Him more and more, a need to become more like Him, a willingness to serve others, a confidence that you are in the best hands, a future with hope and victory, and so on.

I hope and pray that you will want to be closer to God as He wants to be closer to you.

As the deer pants for streams of water, so my soul pants for you, O God. My soul thirsts for God, for the living God. When can I go and meet with God?

Psalm 42:1-2

A SOUND KNOWLEDGE OF YOURSELF

I praise you because I am fearfully and wonderfully made; your works are wonderful, I know that full well.

Psalm 139:14

"I am a 27-year-old female. I have wanted to commit suicide since I have been a teenager. Everything I try or have done turns out to be a failure. I am a homely person, and I have no friends. People think I am strange and a loner. I am looking for the easiest way to kill myself. I have neither the desire, nor the will to live any longer. Life sucks, and I cannot understand why people keep putting children in this pitiful world!"
(This note was posted on the Internet under: Suicide Secrets – Letters and Stories)

My heart aches and goes out to this lady, wishing that I could have a chance to share some truth and good news with anyone who is hurting as the lady who wrote this note was. I don't know if this lady is still alive or not.

Some philosophers have expressed that there are extremely important questions in life, and many have agreed with these three questions:

- Who am I?
- What am I here for?
- Where am I going?

As I ponder these questions, I realize that the first question has to do with **identity**, the second has to do with **purpose**, and the last question has to do with **destiny**. These are very valid questions.

I'm so glad that God in His Word gives us enough light to be able to answer those three questions in a pragmatic and truthful way. Based on what I understand from Scriptures and applying them to my personal life, this is the way I would answer:

- Who am I? I am a child of God created in His image and likeness with a definite and original personality and individuality.
- What am I here for? To know and to love God, to honor and love those close to me, and to be useful with my capacities and talents to serve others, making a difference in this world.
- Where am I going? First to make the most of my life here on earth, then to enjoy eternity in the presence of God.

The Greek philosopher Socrates had an aphorism, *Gnōthi seauton*, which means "Know thyself," or "Know yourself." How important it is to know some facts about ourselves so we don't have to depend on our changing and unpredictable feelings and emotions.

There is a difference between self-image and identity. Self-image has to do with how I value or "appreciate" myself; identity has to do with **who I am**. These two ingredients are intimately related, to the point that one goes with the other, and many times, it is hard to differentiate between the two. Let me just emphasize that the concept we have about ourselves as defining who we are will affect the way we "feel" about ourselves, and will affect our attitudes and actions.

I have a small list describing who we are, according to the Word of God. There are many theories and ideas out there trying to define who we are. As a Christian, my worldview, or my way of thinking, is shaped by what God has to say and not by the popular theories and fads that come and go in this changing and unstable world.

- I am God's creation (Genesis 1:26-27; Psalm 139:13-14).

- I am a beloved child of God (John 1:12; Ephesians 5:1).
- I am a citizen of heaven (Philippians 3:20).
- I am His special treasure (Malachi 3:16-17).
- I am an instrument in His hands (Romans 6:13).
- I am the light of the world (Matthew 5:14).
- I am the salt of the earth (Matthew 5:13).
- I am Christ's ambassador (2 Corinthians 5:20).
- I am a minister of reconciliation (2 Corinthians 5:18).
- I am a royal priest (1 Peter 2:9).
- I am a friend of Christ's (John 15:14-15).
- I am the apple of His eye (Zechariah 2:8).

I'm sure you can add a few more descriptions based on the truth of God's Word.

I recommend you write your own personal statement defining who you are, your purpose in life, and your destiny.

THE SECRET OF CONTENTMENT

But godliness with contentment is great gain. For we brought nothing into the world, and we can take nothing out of it. But if we have food and clothing, we will be content with that.

1 Timothy 6:6-8

Statistics
- 20.7 percent of the world population lived with less than $1 a day in 2004.
- In 2001, 50 percent of the world lived with less than $2.50 a day in 2001.
- According to UNICEF, 26,500 to 30,000 children die per day due to malnutrition and curable diseases.

- Less than 1 percent of what the world spent on weapons in the year 2000 would have put 72 million children in school that year.

The perception of poverty depends a lot on the environment and society where you grew up. The statistics I showed you at the beginning of this theme were meant to help you have a better idea of the realities of this world in which we live.

Some people have noted a difference between needs and wishes, which I believe is correct, but we need to go beyond that because what we may consider a "need" is not necessarily that in a world context.

I grew up in a Third World country and had the privilege of having visited a few other countries and continents, which has affected my perception of poverty. There is a completely different meaning when a teenager in the United States or Europe says, "I need some shoes" than when the same is expressed by a teenager in some parts of Africa, Asia, or Latin America.

There is a great difference between living in a consumer society and living in a surviving society. The difference between extreme poverty and extreme wealth is widening day to day.

The secret of contentment is explained by the apostle Paul in the following passage:

> I am not saying this because I am in need, for I have learned to be content whatever the circumstances. . . . I know what it is to have plenty. I have learned the secret of being content in any and every situation, whether well fed or hungry, whether living in plenty or in want. I can do everything through him who gives me strength.
>
> Philippians 4:11-13

Let me suggest some ingredients to have this secret in your life:

- It is a learning process. It is going to take time to learn and exercise this attitude. Do not expect that in one day, you will "graduate" in contentment. You may need to take just one day at a time, or one test at a time.
- Being satisfied in every circumstance, or the acceptance of your reality, is going to be the key and the goal of this process.
- Gratitude is a must to learn this secret, but not just giving thanks for the good things, but also for the negative circumstances. Let me tell you, if you can be grateful for the adversity that comes your way, then it will be a piece of cake to be grateful for the good things.
- You need to learn to appreciate little things as well as big things. When my younger brother was in the hospital with a growing brain tumor, he was losing his faculties, like his mobility, his sight, and his speech, quite rapidly, then I realized how blessed I was to be able to walk, to see, to talk, to take a shower by myself. I learned to appreciate so many things through his sickness and his death.
- Do you take for granted the air you breathe or your ability to do things at home or at work? Please, don't take anything for granted! Count your blessings because otherwise, you may not realize these blessings until you lose one of them.
- Food, clothing, and shelter are what you really need, and you will be provided for one way or another. Don't worry about that! Just be responsible with what you have at hand, whether it would be your work or your studies; the rest God will provide.

- Take a good look at what you have in your home, and notice how many "extras" you have beyond your needs.
- How do you see things in your life? Some look at a glass filled halfway and say, "It is half empty"; others look at the same glass and say, "It is half full." What do you say?

Is it wrong to want to prosper? Not at all! But if you haven't learned to be content in every circumstance, nothing will be enough for you. What kind of person do you want to be? Now it is up to you.

TRUE WORSHIP

> Yet a time is coming and has now come when the true worshipers will worship the Father in spirit and truth, for they are the kind of worshipers the Father seeks. God is Spirit, and his worshipers must worship in spirit and in truth.
>
> John 4:23-24

In 1984, I was invited to participate in a world congress for Youth for Christ in Hong Kong. Little did I realize that I was going to experience a special moment that would affect me the rest of my life.

Meeting leaders from so many countries was very exciting, the workshops were excellent, and the plenary sessions were inspiring. But the first night, as leaders from all the continents gathered to sing and praise God, it became an overwhelming experience. There is no way to describe it in words, but there was such a sense of the presence of God in that place that I recalled at that moment Peter's experience at the mount of transfiguration, where he said: "Lord, it is good for us to be here. If you wish, I will put up three shelters—one for you, one for Moses and one for Elijah" (Matthew 17:4).

In the same way, I didn't want for that moment to end. I wished it could go on and on. I asked myself, "Why didn't I have an experience like this before? What is it that caused an event like this where God decided to manifest Himself in such a way?" A need to experience God in that way was awakened in the depths of my heart, and I decided to search and research until I would have some specific answers.

So I was reading this passage in John 4, where Jesus is explaining to the Samaritan woman that God is searching for true worshipers, and as I focused my attention to those verses, I started getting some insight from the two expressions Jesus used to qualify a true worshiper: TO WORSHIP IN SPIRIT, AND TO WORSHIP IN TRUTH.

What does it mean to worship in spirit?

We have the ability to communicate with each other on different levels. We say something without too much thought because we are so used to saying the same thing over and over. It is typical in our greetings. We may say, "Hi, how are you?" And the other person may say, "Fine," without thinking enough about what we are saying. In fact, we may not feel fine, but we have already said it. We can sing songs by heart without realizing what we are singing. This superficial and non-thoughtful way of communication is on what is called the mechanical level.

If we want to communicate in a deeper way, then we use our intellectual level. We think and pay attention to what we say, and we are very conscious of what we are saying and listening to.

There is a deeper level of communication, where we express our emotions and feelings. Of course, that reaches to a more intimate part of the person. Our body language, our facial expressions, and our tone of voice participate on this communication level.

Yet, there is even a deeper level, and that is the level of the spirit, where it is more than words and emotions. For instance, the Bible says, "The Spirit himself testifies with our spirit that we are God's children" (Romans 8:16). On many occasions, I have "heard" God speaking to me. It is not an audible voice, but deep inside of me, I know God is saying something very specific to me. It is powerful and undeniable.

So we are able to communicate with God on this deeper level. Words become inadequate to explain, but I know we can develop and grow in communicating with God in this spiritual dimension. As humans, we can communicate with each other heart to heart; as children of God, we can communicate with Him in or through our spirit. Worship, then, can be brought to that level where we can express to God more than what our words, heart, and mind can achieve.

The other characteristic of true worship is worshiping in truth. I submit to you that we can worship in truth in the following ways.

We should worship God according to the truth He has revealed to us about Himself. The more we know and understand every single attribute of Him, the better equipped we will be to honor and exalt Him according to His truth.

The greater our fellowship is with Him, the more we can bask in His presence. We can grow more and more intimate with Him. There is no limit!

Worshiping in truth implies also that we are honest and sincere. Remember, Jesus scolded the teachers of the law for their hypocrisy when He said, "You honor me with your lips, but your hearts are far away from me."

We worship Him in truth when our entire life is devoted to bringing Him praise and honor, and not only those religious moments we call worship. Romans 12:1 says, "Therefore, I urge you, brothers, in view of God's mercy, to offer your bodies as living sacrifices, holy and pleasing to God—this is your spiritual act of worship."

There are many ways we can worship God:

- Expressing thanks and gratitude.
- Exalting His attributes.
- Meditating on Him or on His Word.
- Praying.
- Singing.
- Giving tithes and offerings.
- Reading/studying His Word.
- Having good attitudes.
- Serving/helping others.
- Doing any kind of good actions.
- Working as unto the Lord.
- Enjoying His blessings.
- Being compassionate and merciful.
- Doing our best for His glory in anything we do.
- Talking about Him and His gospel to others.

I hope this list gives you an idea that worship is not just a special moment, but also a lifestyle.

TOTAL SURRENDER THAT LEADS TO HOLINESS

Then he called the crowd to him along with his disciples and said: "If anyone would come after me, he must deny himself and take up his cross and follow me."

Mark 8:34

But just as he who called you is holy, so be holy in all you do; for it is written: "Be holy, because I am holy."

1 Peter 1:15-16

My brother-in-law was traveling one night by bus to another city where he had some business to attend the following day. He was trying to sleep for a little while when suddenly, the bus stopped, and the lights went on. Four men were standing there with automatic weapons pointing at them. The leader of that group said, "Everybody lower your heads and take everything from your pockets and extend your arms to give everything to us, and don't try anything funny because we will kill you right here!"

Everybody took his or her wallet or purse and raised up his or her hands to give the items to the thieves. The leader spoke again: "I want your watches, cell phones, earrings, rings, and necklaces also. Don't try to hide them because we will shoot you." So everybody complied with the request. Some of the passengers were hit on their heads with no reason at all; my brother-in-law was one who was hit.

This was a traumatic experience for him, and he didn't travel by bus for a few years after that. He told me that one of the worst feelings he had was a sense of impotence, not being able to do anything.

He had to surrender under these circumstances, and everything he did for these thieves was against his will.

Many times in our Christian experience, we don't understand the concept of total surrender. Some of us would talk instead of commitment, thinking that this is a really good and noble way of coming to God. Commitment, in some aspects of our lives, is a really good word. For instance, "That person is committed to his work," or, "He is committed to his studies," but when it comes to God, He is completely radical on this, for He says, "Deny yourself, take up your cross, and follow me."

A committed person is still in control of whatever area he is committing to, but God wants total surrender. Maybe that is the reason why there are so many mediocre Christians, so different from first-century Christians, especially in the time of Nero, when being a Christian meant that you may have to give up your life for your faith.

In those days, there was a thirteen-year-old by the name of Marcelo in the city of Rome. He belonged to a distinguished family there, but he had become a Christian. When he was caught for his faith, a Roman centurion said to Marcelo, "For the sake of your family, I am going to give you an opportunity to deny your faith and save your life." But Marcelo was certain of what he believed and answered to the centurion, "I won't give up my faith even if I must die." So the soldiers took Marcelo and threw him to the wild beasts at the Coliseum.

I read in a magazine, *The Voice of the Martyrs*, that in the twentieth century, more Christians have been murdered and tortured than all the martyrs from the first to the nineteenth centuries put together.

The traumatic experience my brother-in-law went through was against his will, and they took away everything he had, leaving him with nothing. But God wants us to surrender to Him voluntarily if we trust Him, and when we do that, He has in store so many blessings for our daily lives and rewards for eternity. I believe this is a nice deal: You give up your imperfect life, and God will transform it for His glory and for your own good, and besides that, He will provide what you really need, and sometimes even more!

We need to reevaluate what it means to be a true Christian. A true Christian is someone who has surrendered his life to God and lives for His glory. That is what literally is meant by the invitation Jesus made to His disciples and the crowd in the verse at the beginning of this subject.

When there is total surrender, there is also total obedience. It does not mean that a Christian does not fail or stumble, but it means that his life has one objective in mind, and that is to walk in the will of God.

If you look from this perspective, you will find that there are many expressions that describe this type of lifestyle:

- A godly life.
- The Spirit-filled life.
- A consecrated life.
- Walking with Christ.
- A walk of obedience.
- Walking in the light.
- A fruitful life.
- The abundant life.
- Living as a true believer.

Peter wrote, "Just as he who called you is holy, so be holy in all you do" (1 Peter 1:15). So basically, everything you do to please God is holiness. God will give you the desire and the ability to experience a lifestyle of holiness; just surrender!

HUMILITY

Take my yoke upon you . . . and you will find rest for your souls.

Matthew 11:29

"True humility is not an abject, groveling, self-despising spirit; it is but a right estimate of ourselves as God sees us."

—Tryon Edwards

"Humility is to make a right estimate of oneself."

—Charles H. Spurgeon

"Humility is the only true wisdom by which we prepare our minds for all the possible changes of life."

—George Arliss

"Sense shines with a double luster when it is set in humility. An able and yet humble man is a jewel worth a kingdom."

—William Penn

"Pride is concerned with *who* is right. Humility is concerned with *what* is right."

—Ezra Taft Benson

Blaise Pascal, a mathematician and philosopher, once expressed it as, "Do you wish people to think well of you? Don't speak well of yourself."

I have included these quotes to provoke your thinking. I think there is a lot of wisdom in what these people had to say.

In most religions, humility is a virtue, and in Christianity, it is not only a virtue, but an indispensable ingredient in salvation; in fact, you cannot enter the kingdom of God without it, and you cannot live the Christian life without humility.

Look with me at two opposing attitudes—the one of Satan, and the one of Jesus:

"You said in your heart, 'I will ascend to heaven; I will raise my throne above the stars of God; I will sit enthroned on the mount of assembly, on the utmost heights of the sacred mountain. . . . I will make myself like the Most High'" (Isaiah 14:13-14). Those were the words of Satan.

"Your attitude should be the same as that of Christ Jesus: Who, being in very nature God, did not consider equality with God something to be grasped, but made himself nothing, taking the very nature of a servant, being made in human likeness. And being found in appearance as a man, he humbled himself and became obedient to death—even death on a cross!" (Philippians 2:5-8).

What a contrast! Satan is proud and arrogant, even though he knows his end, and he will promote his prideful agenda until the end. He is a hopeless, arrogant loser! On the other hand, our Lord and Savior invites us to be humble and meek.

My daughter Joy was asking me, "Dad, what is humility?" I didn't use a definition from a dictionary; instead, I told her, "Honey, humility is knowing who you are for God and being sure of that; you choose to treat and serve others not feeling superior to anyone." And I added, "Without a good self-image, according to God's truth, you cannot be really humble."

Let me tell you what I based that answer on. My first argument comes from Romans 12:3: "For by the grace given me I say to every one of you: Do not think of yourself more highly than you ought, but rather think of yourself with sober judgment, in accordance with the measure of faith God has given you." So the recommendation is to have a sober or sound concept, not one that's higher, but one that's realistic and truthful. Looking down on yourself as a loser or a useless creature is false humility.

Let's confirm this with my second argument: "Jesus knew that the Father had put all things under his power, and that he had come from God and was returning to God; so he got up from the meal, took off his outer clothing, and wraped a towel around his waist. After that he poured water into a basin and began to wash his disciples' feet, drying them with the towel that was wrapped around him" (John 13:3-5).

My take on this is that Jesus was not feeling like less than His disciples. On the contrary, knowing perfectly His glory, He chose to serve others in such a humble and beautiful way. This example makes His command even more appealing and inspiring when He says, "Learn from me, for I am gentle and humble in heart" (Matthew 11:29).

Isn't it wonderful to have a Master who gives us orders, but first models for us and leads the way for us? I want to imitate His lifestyle!

Humility is more an attitude than anything else; therefore, we need to "feed" our soul with thoughts and truthful instruction. When that knowledge becomes our conviction, then we will transpire what is really in the depths of our hearts, and those around us will be able to perceive not our "acting," but a reflection of who we really are.

I want to hate and despise my pride more and more, and cultivate humility more and more. It won't come automatically, but it will grow stronger as I desire to obey and imitate my Lord and Savior. I wish the same for you.

LEARNING TO REST

Come to me, all you who are weary and burdened, and I will give you rest. Take my yoke upon you and learn from me, for I am gentle and humble in heart, and you will find rest for your souls. For my yoke is easy and my burden is light.

Matthew 11:28-30

I was talking to a friend of mine, and he told me, "Johnny, I'm so tired with life. Everything that I'm going through is so overwhelming that I wish I could go to bed and never wake up again." Have you been there? Or maybe you are there right now.

We humans experience all kinds of tiredness, from the simple physical exhaustion after a good game, to the mental fatigue of a student during final tests, or the burnout at a job after a few years of doing something really not liked, or the hopelessness of a bad relationship that is going nowhere, or the burdensome feeling that you are sinking in debt and there is no light at the end of the tunnel.

Let me divide this topic into three parts to help you understand it better: types of tiredness, consequences of unattended tiredness, and the rest we need to have.

We experience four types of tiredness. We can get tired physically, mentally, emotionally, and spiritually. Sometimes we can experience a combination of these types, and sometimes we may experience all of them at once!

Physical tiredness is much easier to understand and deal with. Somehow it is quite obvious, nevertheless, there are many of us who don't pay enough attention to this need and abuse ourselves by forcing ourselves beyond what is prudent, or we keep going without realizing that we may be paying the consequences in our physical bodies or in our interpersonal relationships because we have not been able to discern what a good balance is.

Some workaholics have taken away precious times for bonding and having fun in the family, and instead, they have been working extra time to feel more secure financially. With this I don't mean to negate that there are times when we need to sacrifice something in order to achieve a certain goal or dream. I'm talking primarily about those who have made a habit of sacrificing relationships for the sake of financial success or recognition and acceptance.

Mental tiredness can come as a result of studying a lot, if the amount of information a student is processing is a little too much for his brain. Some could say, "I cannot study one more page, or I will explode!" We know the human brain can take a lot of information and process it—more than what we can imagine. The brain is like a muscle; it will expand its capacity in accordance to its use. But we do get to a limit, when we need a break.

Also, some types of work demand more mental exercise, and by the end of a day, a person can feel exhausted because of the concentration involved. But some of us are not mentally tired because of those reasons; some of us are thinking so much about something that is worrying us, and we can't relax. Many even will experience nightmares, or others, insomnia. They have reached such a level of tiredness that it is becoming more and more difficult to relax and rest.

Emotional tiredness is intimately connected with our way of thinking. If our minds are occupied with negative, pessimistic, frustrating thoughts, then our emotions are going to be directly affected. Bad relationships are going to have a huge impact on our emotions, especially when it comes to those who are close to us. Without resolving and restoring those relationships, it is going to be very difficult to experience rest.

Spiritual tiredness has a lot to do with our bad relationships with others, guilt and shame, a tendency to worry, and a lack of fellowship with God.

The consequences of unattended tiredness are many; let me mention some of them:

- In the physical area, we would lose **productivity**. Everybody knows that a tired person is much less productive than a rested person with lots of energy.
- **Effectiveness** is another area where we can see the results of tiredness. A person with a good energy level is more alert and assertive in any area of work.
- The **mood** is affected by lack of rest, and it is contagious. The opposite is true for those who have had enough rest. Others receive the direct result of your mood, for good or bad. Many companies nowadays emphasize the need to be in a good mood at work in spite of the circumstances one is going through.
- Many **human relations** are damaged by the irritability or hypersensitivity of people who are lacking

rest. Customers can be mistreated by a crabby employee; coworkers will be bothered by a negative attitude. At home, it can be even worse because we can unleash all kinds of negative attitudes and words, with no restraint, in many cases. Some members of the family will keep themselves a prudent distance from a moody person.

- When we don't learn to rest, we develop some **physical problems**, such as ulcers and headaches, just to mention a couple of them. Our body will pay the consequences of our lack of rest. Ask any medical doctor, and he will tell you.
- In some instances, the lack of rest will lead to **emotional and mental problems**. Some people have developed anxiety, panic disorder, depression, and so on.

As you can see, we need to pay more attention to this aspect of rest in our lives. Below, you will find some ideas and suggestions as to how to rest.

Please bear in mind that since we are integrated as a unit, that means whatever we do in the physical, mental, emotional, or spiritual areas affects our whole person. We cannot dissect a person in separate parts; we are an indivisible unit.

- Sometimes just a change of activities can represent a form of rest. I'm sure you have experienced that. For instance, going from working at the office, spending some time in your garden becomes a relaxing and enjoyable time. I used to do that some years ago, and I think I will start doing that again.
- Having a hobby can be so entertaining and relaxing. It is such a rewarding experience to do something

you really like, especially if the work you do is not exciting to you.

• Taking a nap can be the right "recharge" you are looking for. It is better if your nap lasts from fifteen to thirty minutes. If you can do it, I would strongly recommend it.

• Taking a vacation is definitely a time not only to rest and relax, but to have a lot of fun and build good memories with your family.

• Listening to your favorite music or watching a movie can be both relaxing and entertaining.

• Practicing sports or doing physical exercises is another way to bring rest to your life and put your body in good shape.

• Reading a good book can be relaxing, motivating, entertaining, and educational. This is such a good resource we can take advantage of.

• Going out to dinner, a movie, a gathering, a sporting event, or a cultural event can be a gratifying experience. Just make sure you purpose in your heart to enjoy it because I have seen on many occasions how those same things that were meant for our enjoyment can be ruined by someone's negative attitude.

• Talking to someone or looking for counsel from a friend or a professional counselor can bring so much rest and resolution related to so many problems.

• Prayer, Christian fellowship, Bible reading, Bible study, worship, and serving others can become the most rewarding experiences and at the same time can bring so much healing and rest to our lives.

Lastly, I would like to go back to the verses at the beginning of this subject. Here, Jesus is inviting us to come to Him and to put our burdens and worries upon Him, and take the rest He is offering to us. What does it mean in a real and practical sense?

We all experience different kinds of burdens that weigh so heavily on us that we are tired, frustrated, anxious, and even hopeless.

This burden may be a son or daughter going in the wrong direction with a very rebellious attitude when we don't know what else to do. It may be the strain in your marriage, and things are looking really bad at this time. It could be financial stress that you don't see a way out of yet. Maybe there is sickness or a disease that you don't know how to cope with anymore. There could be guilt that you have been bearing for a while now, and you would like to know that there is forgiveness for you. Or it could be one of a host of other burdens.

These are the kinds of burdens Jesus is talking about. You are so limited in what you can do, or probably there is nothing else you can do. Let me tell you with all my heart, this is the perfect time to come to Him. If you can only trust Him, even though you don't see the way out, God is able to open a way where there is none.

During my times of trials, as a reminder of what God is able to do in my life, I remember in Exodus when the Israelites had in front of them the sea and on their backs the army of Pharaoh chasing them. Humanly speaking, there was not a way out, but nobody imagined that God would open the waters of the sea so they could go through on dry land. I have seen how God opens doors when you think you have nowhere else to go.

Without faith it is easy to fall in worry, anguish, and desperation, but you can find rest and hope. Sometimes it is not that we will receive the petition that we are asking for, but His peace, which surpasses all understanding, and sometimes He will give us even more of what we have asked for.

SPIRITUAL DISCIPLINES

> Everyone who competes in the games goes into strict training. They do it to get a crown that will not last; but we do it to get a crown that will last forever.
>
> 1 Corinthians 9:25

Don't you envy the shape and the ability of an Olympic athlete? I wish I could be in that kind of shape! It is only a wish at my age!

I would like to compare the virtues in a Christian to the muscles of an athlete, and I would like to call them "spiritual muscles" because the muscles of an athlete don't happen by accident; instead, they are the result of hard, educated, and consistent training.

If salvation is free, why do we have to put ourselves in such a discipline? Because while we live on earth, we are in constant battles with forces that want to destroy us and make our faith look like a ridiculous spectacle of a religion of fanatical people with no brains, who are following a myth and are a bunch of complete losers.

When these forces see true Christianity, they may attempt to contradict our beliefs, but they cannot deny what they see with their own eyes, and some of them are waiting for our example because they would like to have the hope and the joy we experience. They want to see something that really works, and that is a transformed life, which in the darkness of this world becomes a shining light.

Another reason to embrace this discipline is because God wants to shape in each of us the image of His Son, Jesus Christ, and that image is perfect and beautiful.

One more argument I would like to mention is that for every effort we make here to bring glory to God, He will reward us generously in heaven for eternity.

And let us not forget that the first beneficiaries of a good lifestyle are us; we will harvest blessings, peace, joy, and honor. This is the smartest investment you can make, where there is no possibility of losing, no risk involved!

What are the disciplines that would shape us and make us strong and healthy in our spiritual life?

- **Simple obedience.** It starts with plain and simple obedience because if we start disobeying simple commands, we are not going to be able to understand when things become more complicated. Like in math, you have to start with simple operations of addition, subtraction, division, and multiplication with single digits, then you will get more and more complicated assignments that will involve fractions and decimals, and later on, you will be dealing with algebra and equations and so on.
- **Christian fellowship or church attendance** is another discipline we need to cultivate in our lives. It will help us learn from other believers the things of God, will be our support and encouragement, and will give us the opportunity to share and to grow in different areas.
- **Bible study and Bible reading.** Learn by yourself and with the help of others about God and His perfect will for your life. You will discover so many things, and it will give you the ability to differentiate more and more between right and wrong.
- **Prayer.** You will be able to talk to God about anything. That communication directly with God will be your opportunity to spend time with God whenever you want to and whenever you need to. You will experience the freedom to express your doubts, your anguish, your needs, your gratitude, and your victories; to intercede for others; to ask for help; and so on. You will sense God's closeness to you, and you

will see that there is an amazing Source of power and strength that you can unleash through prayer.

- **Worship.** This discipline will help you to express and to celebrate your relationship with God. You will be able to contemplate His glory, to enjoy His presence, and to praise and thank Him for who He is, for what He has done, for who He is in your life, for what He will do, and so on. If you want to experience a piece of heaven on earth, this is the discipline that will provide that blessing.

- **Service.** You will discover that there is more meaning and purpose in life as you get out of yourself and invest your time, talents, and treasure in service to others. To your amazement, you will discover that there is incredible joy in serving others, much more than money can buy.

- **Testimony.** In this discipline, even though it is a little uncomfortable at the beginning, you will discover that sharing with others about God, His Word, and His salvation not only rescues people from hell, but transforms lives and gives you such a joy that you won't be able to express it in words. Helping people find God is the best favor you can do for anyone. Of course, this includes the testimony you share without words by your lifestyle.

Let me wrap up this point with a couple of verses that Paul wrote:

Have nothing to do with godless myths and old wives' tales; rather, train yourself to be godly. For physical training is of some value, but godliness has value for all things, holding promise for both the present life and the life to come.

1 Timothy 4:7-8

A GREAT EXPECTATION

I consider that our present sufferings are not worth comparing with the glory that will be revealed in us.

Romans 8:18

Let's say the company you work for has decided to send you and your family on a vacation for a whole week, with all expenses paid, of course, and even some extra cash for shopping, and your destination is Disney World. You have three days to prepare your luggage and clothes for this trip, and since your plane leaves at 6 A.M. you and your family will have to get up at least by 4 A.M. in four days.

What do you think would be the reaction of your spouse and kids? Would they complain that they have to prepare their suitcases? Or that they have to get up so early? I would venture to say that, in most cases, the answer would be no! The excitement is so overwhelming that they wouldn't mind "sacrificing" their sleep or working to pack their suitcases. They won't even complain if their suitcase is too heavy!

That is precisely one of the motivations for our lives! Eternal glory is waiting for us! We have some description of what it is going to be like getting "there," so let's look at some of that, but bear in mind that it is only a partial view because it is going to be much more than what I'll describe.

The place is called the City of God. It has streets of gold, the gates of the city are huge pearls, and the walls of the city are made with precious stones, and that is just the beginning.

It will be a perfect place, with no sickness or death, no wars, no fights, no more suffering, no more pain, no more injustice or unfairness, no more good-byes of loved ones, no more loss, no more confusion, no more despair. It is the place we all long for.

Peace, love, joy, and kindness are all over there. No one is trying to be first; there's no more competing, so you won't lose. There's no more rejection, no more hate. All are accepted; no one is less. Isn't that the place to be?

The glory of God fills the place. There's no need for the sun or the moon because God is there, and you will see Him face to face.

There is no hurry in that place. Everybody has plenty of time for you; no one needs to go. There you will visit with Moses, Elijah, King David, and Solomon. You will have the luxury to visit with your heroes of old and all the heroes that you never knew about, and maybe for some of them you are a hero, too.

You will be recognized there for a work well done, and before all the angels and all the saints there, you will receive in public a gold crown, and Jesus will stand there smiling at you and will say, "Well done, good and faithful servant; enter into the joy of the Lord!"

Until that day comes, live in a way that others may find what you have, and they will honor you by wanting to be just like you.

A final note about thinking positively. This was the counsel of God through His servant Paul:

Finally, brothers, whatever is true, whatever is noble, whatever is right, whatever is pure, whatever is lovely, whatever is admirable—if anything is excellent or praiseworthy—think about such things.

Philippians 4:8

What is the legacy you will leave behind?

May God bless you!

I would like to share with you a chart I wrote for myself on June 1, 1997. That was and still is the expression of my heart, will, and soul. I am now reaffirming with you, in a nutshell, what my life is all about.

PURPOSE AND MEANING

My highest experience	To know Him personally
My highest privilege	To serve Him
My highest honor	To die for Him
My highest reward	To contemplate His glory
My highest goal	To be like Him
My motivation	My love for Him
My confidence	Jesus in me
My source of power	His Holy Spirit
My rest	His grace
My philosophy in life	Apart from Him, I can do nothing.
My reason for living	To bring Him glory

Printed in the United States
217328BV00001B/235-426/P